My Dear Old Glasgow Years

My Dear Old Glasgow Years

Walter Bernardini

Fort Publishing Ltd

First published in 2018 by Fort Publishing Ltd,
12 Robsland Avenue, Ayr, KA7 2RW

Walter Bernardini has asserted his rights under
the Copyright, Designs and Patents Act, 1988 to
be identified as the author of this work.

Typeset by Hewer Text UK Ltd, Edinburgh
Cover graphics by Mark Blackadder
Cover painting by Walter Bernardini

ISBN: 978-1-905769-60-5

Printed by Totem.com.pl

I dedicate this book to my darling wife Tina,
whose memory lives within my heart and throughout these pages.

Contents

Preface

Having been a designer and artist all my life, writing a book did not come naturally. That all changed in 2017 on the passing of my wife, after fifty-nine years together. It was sad to watch her suffer from dementia and decline over a nine-year period, during which time I became her full-time carer. After her death, my grieving process was tinged with a certain amount of freedom, which I hadn't experienced for some time. I thought painting might in some way relieve my depression, but it didn't really help. It was then that I came across a Facebook group, comprising mostly of people born in Glasgow and now worldwide emigrants. The person who oversees the group is a man called Norry Wilson and I owe him a debt of gratitude, not only for accepting me into the group but also for monitoring it with such dedication and precision.

I posted my first insignificant, as I thought, piece of memorabilia over a year ago and since then I have been flooded with positive comments for more of the same, things like 'can't wait for the next episode' and 'this should be a book'. Acting upon this last suggestion, the following pages attempt to give the reader an account of the most meaningful events in my life over a thirty-year period. Every word is a true recollection of my experiences, good or bad, during that time.

I have so many people to thank for their support, encouragement and guidance, both meaningful, in a literal sense, and technical. The latter is my youngest daughter Alison's area of expertise and as she lives closest to me, is on hand to keep me right. I am also indebted to her for all her help during the later stages of my wife's illness, when I became less able to cope. At this stage, it would be remiss of me not to thank my other two daughters, Linsey and Janis, for their constant supervision and attention by phone and by e-mail from across the sea. Thank you both so much.

To all my lovely friends in the Lost Glasgow Group, with whom I am now in regular contact, I also owe a huge debt of gratitude. Their friendship has enabled me to come to terms with the loss of my wife, and afforded me access to a worldwide group of people, something I could never have imagined eight months ago.

So now it's over to you, the reader. I hope you enjoy my ramblings.

Walter Bernardini
Dublin, November 2018

Childhood

Early Years

This collection of short stories and anecdotes begins in the 1920s and takes us through hard times, sad times and glad times up to and including 1963 when I departed Scotland to begin a new life in the Republic of Ireland.

Many historic events took place in the Twenties: *The Jazz Singer*, starring Al Jolson, heralded the end of the silent movies; jazz and ragtime were becoming popular, flappers were all the rage, the Charleston being the most popular dance; Charles Lindbergh made the first solo transatlantic flight in his monoplane, *The Spirit of St Louis*; Joseph Stalin took control of Russia from Lenin; the sculpting of four American presidents at Mount Rushmore began. Many more events were to take place in that decade, none of which could compare with the ones I have mentioned. But I would like to draw attention to one of those insignificant events, because it plays a vital role in my story. On 4 February 1927, Jeannie Lightbody and Peter Bernardini, both from Tollcross, were married. At that time, my father worked as an electrician in Stewarts & Lloyds and my mother worked in the Danish dairy; no, not in Denmark, but across the street from where she lived. (I can only assume that it was called the 'Danish' dairy because they sold butter imported from Denmark.)

It took them five years to get around to having their only son: me! I am thankful they did, otherwise you wouldn't be reading this now.

I was born on the last day of January in Rottenrow hospital, so named because of the street on which it was located. Rottenrow became its rather unfortunate nickname, since the days when it was a 'lying-in' hospital for women in the 1830s. It was given its more respectable title when moving premises in 1860 and thenceforth became known as the Glasgow Royal Maternity hospital.

We lived at 592 Shettleston Road, my parents' second house, their first one being opposite Janefield cemetery near Parkhead. My recollections from those early years are vague but there are some facts I can relate. My maternal grandad, James Lightbody, worked as a cabinet maker at John Brown's shipyard and crafted many pieces of furniture for the *Queen Mary*, some of which, I believe, are still in existence and can be seen in the on-board staterooms at her moorings in Long Beach, California. Being an employee, he was allocated tickets to attend the launch, as were many other men who had worked on the ship. Not that I remember, but I believe I was carried there in my mother's arms as I was still only two years old. There was a long-held belief that any time royalty visited Glasgow, it rained. Well Glasgow lived up to its reputation that day because when the Queen came to launch the ship that was to bear her name, it poured, and the umbrellas went up. The launch was the end of a long process; it had been four long years since the ship's keel was laid and given the hull number, 534. But work was suspended for a year in 1931 due to the Great Depression. The enthusiastic crowd of onlookers, wives, workers and relatives had waited so long for this day and were rewarded by seeing hull 534 finally given a name and taken to the water at last.

One night I was awakened by my dad, who carried me over to the window to see a great luminous shape moving majestically across the Glasgow sky. This, I'm told, was the Graf Zeppelin on one of her transatlantic flights and it was a sight that made so great an impression that I can visualise it today, in my eighty-sixth year. My mother made her displeasure known about my father's well-intentioned nocturnal disturbance, and, truth be told, I was glad to get back to sleep.

One of my first pranks was at age three. I decided to hide under the bed, which was high enough off the floor to accommodate my wee frame and I sat bolt upright and well out of sight. I stayed there, quiet as a mouse, counting the bedsprings above my head and enjoying every minute of my prank. The longer it lasted, the happier I was. I could hear my mother's voice calling my name all around the house as she looked for me. 'Oh, there you are,' as the bedclothes were pulled up to reveal my beaming countenance. I'm sure she knew I had been there all the time, but it seemed to me that I had pulled off the surprise of the week.

I loved springing surprises, but the tables were turned on Christmas morning later that year. I had already seen what was in my stocking; a coloured ball, an apple and a string bag with chocolate coins wrapped in gold foil inside. But I had a sixth sense there was something else, and, as I quickly turned round, there it was: a big, square box carefully wrapped in Christmas paper. Judging by the size, it must have been the present I had asked Santa to bring. I was on the floor, impatiently tearing the paper off, when suddenly, above my head, my mother let out a scream as she caught sight of something moving above the fireplace. It was a real live puppy, which, until now, had remained very still and very quiet. My father had put him inside my helmet and hung it from string tied to each side of the mantelpiece. It made my Christmas, although I can't say the same for my mother. She was more concerned about the practical problems of owning a dog. Who would take him for walks? What about those wee jobbies and pees he would be leaving behind while he was being trained?

We named the pup Ruffy. My father loved wire-haired terriers for their clean lines, smart appearance, smooth coat and upright tail. Unfortunately, he had been sold something of a pup, if you'll excuse the pun, and a hairier variety of pup at that. As I say, this didn't go down too well with my mum; she was thinking about the hair she would have to clean up. However, he was mine and I loved him, even more than my train set, for a while at least.

My granny came over later that day.

'Look what Santa brought, Granny,' I said, lifting Ruffy to show her.

'Oh, that was very good of Santa,' she replied, harbouring the same practical thoughts as my mother. Their misgivings were understandable; our close opened directly onto a busy main road. My granny had brought me a big, red, clockwork motor car, which, when fully wound up, could run fast, even over the carpet. I liked the car but it was Ruffy who was the centre of attention that Christmas morning.

Just along the back at 592, and down from the middens, there was a great wee area for playing on. It was quite sandy and me and my pals would scrape out roads for our Dinky motors to run on. We would have great fun racing our cars and crashing them into one another. When we got fed up with that, we would go up the street that ran alongside the back and up to a big, square opening in the wall at the side of Shettleston baths. There we could gather for a heat from the great open furnace, which had red-hot coals burning with a lovely red glow. The heat, as you can imagine, was fierce but then it had to be to heat the water for the steamie. I would always think, 'that's what hell must look like down there'.

The only thing that stopped you from falling into the hot coals was a big metal bar running across the front, with a gap you could fall through if you weren't careful. Davy Chester, one of our pals, was always one for doing dokeys; that's where you would 'tumle yer wulkies' or jump up on dykes with both feet together, to show off. He decided to jump up on the bar and turn head first with the intention of swinging back to land beside us on the pavement. It didn't go to plan, but we were relieved that he didn't fall into the jaws of hell. Somehow, we managed to pull him back onto the pavement, thereby avoiding a toss-up to decide who would be breaking the news of his incineration to his mammy.

Another great event at that time was the scramble. No, not the motorbike scrambles they have nowadays. Scrambles took place when a bride was being taken to church in the car; her father, travelling with her, was expected to throw a bunch of coins out to us kids, as we eagerly waited, hands outstretched. One time, a bride up the next close was on her way to church and the coins were duly thrown out. I was one of the hopefuls and when the money was in the air the scramble was on. Her daddy must have been saving up for weeks because the air was thick with pennies and by the time the car sped off the money was all over the road, never mind the pavement. Unable to resist, I got down on my hands and knees like the rest of them but as I was filling my pockets I heard a shout from our window.

'Walter!'

It was my mother.

'Come up here this minute.'

When I got into the house, there was no, 'Thank goodness ye didnae get run over.' Oh no! In my eagerness to grab my share of the loot, I had run onto the road and that was a criminal offence.

'Come here,' my father shouted. I could tell he meant business because the strap was out. That instrument of torture was the strap he used to sharpen his open razor. It was only used on serious occasions.

'Bend doon. *Don't* . . . let me . . . *see* . . . you running . . . *oot* . . . *ontae* . . . that . . . *road* . . . again.'

Five whacks, each one timed to emphasise a word.

'D'ye hear?' he concluded, giving me a final whack for luck.

No such luck for me though. Tears streaming down my cheeks I ran and threw myself on top of the bed, nursing a sore bum. After the waterworks subsided, I checked my pockets. Thank goodness, I still had my money.

The memories from 592 are vivid. I can remember my father taking me down to Shettleston station to see the trains. They were local trains of course, but, to me, the engines were huge and sometimes we would venture up to where they had stopped. I thought that my dad knew every engine driver there was, because he would engage the driver in conversation, whilst nodding in my direction, and the driver would always take the wink.

'Hello son. I hear you want tae be an engine driver. Good boy.' That would be enough to cement the relationship between us men. According to his disposition, he might even give a wee toot on his whistle just to show me the power he had as a driver.

Sometimes we would be treated to a tank engine on its own, trundling past on its way back to the shed for the night. Tank engines were the ones without a tender for the coal, and had a simple wheel arrangement of 4:4:2. The rods attached to the four big driving wheels would make a 'stallia, stallia, stallia' sound as they passed, bringing my musical ear into action, although which ear it was I never found out. I went back home a happy bunny.

Life was as good as it could be back then but one day my parents had had an awful row over something of which I wasn't aware. Such was the rift between them that my father was shown the door in no uncertain terms. Separation or divorce were words that weren't in my vocabulary but they could easily have been applied in this case. My father grabbed me by the hand and whisked me downstairs to get a tram into town.

When we got there, we seemed to be wandering around aimlessly, and in silence, until we ended up somewhere he felt at ease. It was an Italian food shop owned by the Fazzi brothers, which was down a side street off the Gallowgate. It wasn't as if my father spoke Italian, although he often talked about joining the Italian institute. *Burro* (butter), *asuccaro* (sugar) and *choccolata* were about the stretch of his Italian, words he would use frequently at home, as though he was a native. In Fazzis', large, sausage-shaped salamis of every shape and size hung invitingly from hooks suspended from the roof and the smell was even more enticing. He made his purchases but didn't need to bring his pidgin Italian into play. After all, we didn't need *burro* or *choccolato* and anyway all the assistants spoke a quasi Scots-Italian akin to Grampa Bernardini in his ice-cream shop in Tollcross.

He bought a box of sweeties for my mammy, a gesture of reconciliation. Not flowers mind, as he would have felt a right pansy carrying them on the car and would have got funny looks from the other passengers. Our journey home was punctuated by little more conversation than on the journey into town. We went up the stairs and into a quiet house, so quiet you could hear the clock ticking on the mantelpiece.

'Here you are Jean,' he said, handing over the sweeties. 'A brought you these.'

His peace offering was accepted without so much as a thank you, never mind conciliatory kisses or hugs. That would have been a step too far considering the circumstances. In fact, under any circumstances. In those days, displays of affection weren't the done thing.

'Oh an' a got some pasta and salami while we were in town. We can always do wi' that can't we?'

A wee smile from my mother was all I needed to detect the return of a degree of marital harmony; I wouldn't be getting packed off to an orphanage after all. Relations between my parents were much more secure than I had imagined. Indeed, I never again heard them at each other's throats.

I began to hear murmurings of us moving from 592 behind my back. If that happened, our expansion plans would come to nothing. You see, my best pal, Eddie Mitchell, lived through the wall from us and we both had a train set. Now during one of our sleepovers we had a great idea. If we could only dig a tunnel between the two houses and join up the rails we would have an inter-house rail link in no time. At that age, of course, it never crossed our minds how our houses were built; there would be at least four feet of concrete to dig out before we could even lay the track. So, after much deliberation, we scrapped the idea. After all, where could we get a pickaxe at that time of night? After a lot of giggling we drifted into the land of make believe and 'couried doon' for the night.

There was a woman who stayed three stairs up, next close to us, called Mrs McWhinnie. She lived alone and the poor woman was deaf. Every so often she would make a panful of fritters. You might ask, how did I know that? No, she didn't make them for herself, she made them for us weans, simply because she enjoyed watching us eat them. When we heard her window go up, we knew there was a treat in store.

'Who's furst?' she would bellow.

Silly question, because the combined roar was always deafening.

'Me, me, me, Mrs McWhinnie. Me!'

Now she may have been hard of hearing but she knew how to control a crowd. Especially a hungry crowd like us.

'Line up,' she'd shout. 'Wee Audrey furst.'

That was Audrey McKinnon from the last close. She was what would be termed today a special-needs child. Sure enough, Audrey would be pushed to the front of the queue and when her wrapped fritter was thrown out, no matter who caught it, wee Audrey was always handed it because we knew Mrs McWhinnie was watching. Everybody waited their turn and in due course received their fritters, wrapped carefully in brown paper. If nothing else, Mrs McWhinnie was fastidious about cleanliness. Come to think of it, her bill for potatoes and lard must have amounted to a good bit every week. But feeding us hungry kids was one of the joys of her life. God bless her.

All too soon, the talk about the move to Tollcross became a reality. I don't remember much about the flitting because that was big people's work; I was lifted and laid with no questions asked. Granny Lightbody's sister, Jean, had 'married into money', as they used to say, and she persuaded her husband Andrew – who happened to be the owner of A. & R. Muir & Sons, well- known sculptors at that time – to set my aunt May up in business running a newsagent's shop at 377 Clarkston Road. There was a room and kitchen, with bathroom no less, on the first landing above the shop. My aunt May had always worked for Brown's the newsagents, across from where they stayed in Tollcross Road and this was a great chance to run her own shop on the other side of Glasgow. A new beginning for her and the family and a new house for the three of us. Mind you, we didn't have the luxury of a bathroom, not that we did at 592.

Only the one toilet on the landing, shared between the three families that lived there. At least we had our own lavvy key!

I don't remember much about my first day at Wellshot school, which was within walking distance of our house. I remember my mother taking me and because I was only five, for the first few days she used to come back at playtime with a wee piece. I would, on occasion, try to share it with Nessie McBride, the first girl I had a crush on; well not so much her, more her coat. You see, she had this fur coat that I wanted to be near and to touch. Nessie McBride lived in a big house in Drumover Drive, as I was later to find out, because a good few years after that I was invited to a party there. Nothing ever came of the love affair with the coat. I was shunned on that first encounter and by the time of the party the coat was long gone. The party was a respectable affair, with the usual balloons and games for her young friends and relations. Many years later, when I was in my teens, I found out that the same Nessie had become a constable with Glasgow police and was working in Pollokshaws.

Back to Wellshot. Desks in the infant classes were laid out on the same level, with a wee space between them. As we moved into the next and subsequent classes, the desks were arranged in tiers, which rose step by step until you reached the back row. The term 'top of the class' meant exactly that, not only because of the number of steps it took to get up there, but also due to the brainpower it took to stay there. It didn't take me long to figure that out; work hard, stay up, was the motto.

I took to my schooldays quite well, and, for the most part, enjoyed them, especially when we heard the rattle of milk bottles. Every day we quenched our thirsts from one of those dainty wee bottles with the cardboard tops and when they were empty they would be put back in the crate. Only then were you let out for playtime, a mixture of rough and tumble for the boys and skipping ropes and beds marked out with chalk for the girls. When playtime was over, we formed into lines and went back to our classes.

Our teachers were generally nice and, especially in infant class, lenient. Only when we grew up did it become apparent who was boss. Mrs Clark was the strictest, probably because she was married and spent half the time wondering what she would get for her man's tea. Miss Ogilvie on the other hand was always smiling and looked as if she really liked us. She was a kind soul and every Friday without fail she stood at the door with a lovely smile and a bag of cinnamon balls, letting us pick one when we left. They were an acquired taste, but I loved them, and her too. Was this another crush?

What a difference to Mrs Reid, who took our next class. She stood no nonsense from anyone. One day, a bunch of pens tied with an elastic band round them had been placed on a front desk ready for composition while the inkwells were filled. It happened to be where Gordon Livingstone sat. Gordon was the wild one in our class, always making trouble. He must have had ringworm because his head was completely shaven, making him a dead ringer for Genghis Khan, which didn't help. Mrs Reid and Gordon must have had a serious disagreement that day, because he lifted the bunch of pens and flung it in her direction with all his might. Fortunately, the projectile missed by inches and was impaled on the blackboard behind her, only to fall limply to the floor because of its weight.

It was the final straw. Mrs Reid grabbed Gordon by the lug and marched him down to Mr Gilmour, the headmaster, whose office was situated at the Shettleston end of the school. I can only imagine the scene. Burned at the stake would have been an appropriate punishment in the olden days but, even from our classroom, we could hear six of the belt, on crossed hands, being administered. Come on, child abuse or no, that was what he should have expected for attempted murder. Class dismissed at the end of the day, we marched out to an appropriate song played on the piano at the end of the hall by one of the musically accomplished teachers.

'We'll make a bonfire of our troubles and then we'll watch them fade away,' the song went.

Very appropriate, as poor Gordon's hands must have been burning.

Christmas and New Year

We didn't celebrate Christmas much in our house. Santa Claus, of course, present giving and perhaps a clootie dumpling; that was it. But there is one Christmas story I would like to share. My mother decided to ask my granny and grandad, Aunt May and Uncle Jack over for Christmas dinner. She had managed to persuade my father to take the annual present of a turkey from the GEC at Christmas instead of New Year, a real sacrifice for Dad because he loved his Ne'erday turkey. The family arrived and had settled down for a pre-meal drink: a dram for grandad, a beer for uncle Jack and a sweet sherry for granny and my aunt May. Then we sat down to eat.

Santa had given me a microphone and I had learnt how to use it. My dad, an electrician by trade, connected it up in such a way that I could speak into it with the sound coming through the wireless in the kitchen, where everybody was seated. I had set up a wee prank to play on our guests, in particular my granny. She liked to listen to the Queen's Christmas broadcast, so I decided to fill in for Her Majesty. I was good at accents and impersonations, and my voice, still unbroken, was also a help. During the enjoyment of the meal, the dumpling and the paper hats and all that, the real Queen's speech had come and gone. So, once I got my sixpence wrapped in greaseproof paper out of the dumpling I skipped away to the room and got set up. Mum and Dad were in on the joke; all I had to do was to listen for my cue.

'Oh, the Queen's broadcast, we've missed it,' my granny moaned. She knew it always came on at three o' clock and it was now quarter to four.

Mum played her part to perfection.

'No, I think it's later this year ma. She might still be speakin'.'

'Ye never know,' my dad interjected.

That was my cue. I broke in, making it sound as if she was nearing the end of the broadcast.

'. . . and to all of my people, especially those of you who are listening throughout the Commonwealth, I wish you all a very merry Christmas. Speaking to you from Sandringham, surrounded by my family, it gives me very special pleasure to send Christmas greetings this year to you, Lizzie Lightbody, who I know is visiting her daughter Jean, up there in Tollcross, Glasgow.'

Our guests, sitting around the kitchen table, were stunned. My granny exclaimed, 'Oh my michty me. Oh goodness me. Is she speakin' tae me? Who telt her a wis here?'

16

Time for me to leave my microphone and run through to the kitchen.

'It was me Granny. It was me.'

I was so proud that my microphone had done its job. It wouldn't have been Christmas without the Queen's speech.

For Boxing Day, it was over to my granny's house above the shop in Cathcart. She had just about recovered from the message from the Queen, and this would turn out to be a very different type of celebration. Dinner was in a crammed kitchen, which could barely accommodate seven, even with someone sitting on the bed. There was much passing round of plates over heads, but we managed to get through it fine.

When everybody had eaten, and were trying to look festive in those silly hats made of tissue paper, it was time to go through to the room. My mother and aunt May were left at the sink, washing and drying the dishes and rejecting Granny's offer of help; she was better out the road. We were sitting comfortably and the fruit was brought in for afters, as if we needed anything else after such a big meal.

'Can a look at the war books please?' I had to ask nicely because the said war books were a treasured library of nine, heavily bound, red volumes, liberally illustrated with photographs from the First World War. I was happy with two at a time, as they were heavy. Meanwhile, everyone else was enjoying a game using cards split into two lots, with questions on one and answers on the other. Quite naughty too if the oohs and aahs as they were being read out were anything to go by. Then came the apples, and one orange, which had been divided into scliffs; it was wartime after all. The pieces were handed out with one or two chocolates as a wee treat.

Next up was party time.

'Come on Jack. Give us a tune.' There was a piano against the wall, opposite the fireplace; it had been bought for him and he guarded it with his life. It reeked of furniture polish, lovingly and regularly lashed on by aunt May. Uncle Jack had played the organ in his younger days, but was sadly out of practice. Despite that, after much persuasion, he flexed his fingers, pulled out the piano stool and selected his standard recital piece, the identity of which came as no surprise to the assembled company.

Off he went: 'dum de dum, de de de de de, dum de dum, diddly dum dum dum de dum, de de de de de, dum de dum'. Now those of you with any knowledge of classical music will have guessed it – the *Polonaise in A*, by Fredric Chopin. His rendition was punctuated throughout by many oops, and still more oops, as the wrong keys were played. Polite applause however, and a yawn from me; I would much rather have heard some boogie woogie, which, when no one else was in the room, I would try to hammer out on the sacred piano.

Now it was May's turn. 'Oh, all right then,' she agreed, without, it must be said, much coaxing. She gestured to Jack, who would be her accompanist on the piano, and he got out the sheet music for her song. With hands clasped in front and a wee clearing of the throat, she launched into her party piece. 'Cherry ripe, cherry ripe, ripe, I cry . . .' she sang. While this was going on I had just reached 'The Battle of Vimy Ridge' in the war book.

The little soiree wouldn't have been complete without a tune on the fiddle from my grandad. Sure enough, the fiddle was carefully lifted from its place on the kitchen wall, given a wee dust by aunt May, and brought through. Of course, some time elapsed as he plinked and plonked and twisted the knobs to get it in tune but when he eventually got going he wasn't too bad, considering his age and the fact that it had been hanging on the wall for a year. There were a few bum notes – let's put it down to poor tuning – but his performance was also received with the obligatory once-a-year clap.

'Come on noo, Walter, we know you can sing,' someone said, keen that I join in. And this, just as a Sopwith Camel was about to shoot down a Fokker Triplane.

'Oh, a cannae sing,' I lied.

'What about that one you did at Mabel Neil's concert?' my mother asked.

'Och that was a duet. An' a would need ma tap shoes for that.'

Not, mind you, that they would have been any good on the carpet.

It did the trick; I was let off this time. Besides it was getting late and nearly time for us to go for the car. The couch we were sitting on was required as it had then to be pulled out and turned into a bed where my grandad and Uncle Jack slept.

New Year was always special. The first time I was allowed to stay up for 'the bells' was the start of a great romance; no one in the world can compare with we Scots in the love of New Year. There was a wee dairy up the road called Jenny Dougall's, where my mother bought treacle scones, potato scones and Paris buns. I used to ask myself if they came all the way from Paris but it really didn't matter because they tasted so good thanks to those wee grains of sugar on top, which were great to lick.

My mum and dad had become friends with Jenny and her husband, Jimmy, and had been invited to 'first foot' them that

New Year. At Hogmanay, our house had to be spotless, including the grate, which had to be black-leaded, and everything else that could be polished, left shining. I remember my father jokingly referring to himself as Peter the Great because at New Year my mother would take considerable delight in brandishing the tin and reminding him, 'Right Peter, the grate!'

The Hogmanay ritual was always the same. As midnight approached my mother would open the door to let the 'auld year oot'. My father would leave before twelve, remembering to close the door behind him, and taking his bottle with him, as well as something to bring in for the 'hoose' to make sure he was the first foot over the door as the New Year arrived. Then there was the 'knock, knock' – ringing the bell was deemed to be bad luck. My mother opened the door to 'Happy New Year' as my father crossed the threshold, presenting his gift for the hoose.

That was the ritual of first-footing. If some wee blondie woman, instead of a tall dark man, was to rush in later without a gift, it wouldn't matter. He would still have been the first foot, bringing his luck and best wishes for the year ahead, and, believe it or not, it is a tradition I follow to this day. Then after the customary 'tak' in and gie oot' of drinks between visitor and resident – they never could decide which came first – as well as a wee finger of shortbread or slice of black bun, we were ready to go out and do our first footing.

On my 'first' New Year it was snowing slightly as we walked up the road but we didn't have far to go. Past the shop on the main street, around the corner and into the lane leading to the door of their house. There was a 'mind and wipe yer feet' from my mother as we entered the house, my father first, of course, with his bottle and 'Happy New Years' all round. Jenny and Jimmy had a big wall clock with a loud pendulum that I couldn't help staring at. 'Tick . . . tock . . . tick . . . tock . . . New . . . Year . . . New . . . Year,' it seemed to say. The other thing I couldn't help noticing: Jenny's hair! It was the first time I had seen her without the 'granny much' hat she always wore while serving in the shop and for once she looked presentable. Well, it was New Year.

'Wid ye like another wee glass o' ginger wine son?'

'Yes please.'

I was getting the hang of all this drinking, but there was no singing or carousing. Just quiet, big people's conversation. New Year can be like that, especially if close friends or relatives have passed on during the past twelve months. My sense of anticipation had been building for some time and I was ready for something quite exciting, but it was a dull evening, except for that bloody clock. 'Tick . . . tock . . . tick . . . tock.'

New Year. Was that it? Surely the next one would be better.

Tollcross years

1060 Tollcross Road was such a change from our old house in Shettleston. We were going to be staying in a house that was three stairs up. I had often been to the house, on visits to my granny and grandad, but this was where we were going to live for ever, and from now on it would be home. A simple room and kitchen with a long counter beneath the windows and a sink at the opposite end from the food press. The fireplace was contained within the grate and this, in turn, heated the water and provided heat for cooking. The pulley, which hung from the ceiling, had a distinctive squealing sound when it was in use. The bunker was in the lobby and had cupboards next to it, where I could keep my toys, and at the end of the lobby there was a tall press. My bed, which had a recess, was in the front room. My mother and father slept in the kitchen in their hole-in-the-wall bed, directly through the wall from mine.

This description will sound familiar to those of you who lived, or were brought up in, similar houses, but it might bring back memories of Glasgow at that time. The front-room window looked over the Vale's park, with Shettleston and the sand quarry beyond. From the kitchen, you could see over the back green, which was fenced off with four washing-line posts at either end. Over the wall from the wash house and the bin space was the well-tended cemetery, much visited on Sundays, adjoining the Central church, and, further still, Clyde Iron Works. Beyond that again we had an expansive view, taking in the Cathkin braes, which stretched down past Dixon's Blazes, and ended with the familiar shape of Rutherglen town hall. There were also three distinctive tree formations on the Cathkins, in the middle, just above Cambuslang. In my childhood imaginings they were HMS *Nelson*, while on top of the hills I saw a camel and a buffalo.

These tree formations have changed over the years. I was a passenger in my daughter's car driving past the scene while on a return visit to Scotland, some seventy-five years later, and while HMS *Nelson* had become indiscernible due to a change in growth patterns, the camel is still there and what could pass for a buffalo or a bison could also be seen on the horizon. It brought back my childhood and you can call me a romantic old git if you like, but as Clark Gable said to Vivien Leigh in *Gone with the Wind*, 'Frankly, my dear, I don't give a damn.'

I had been making such a racket on my tin drum that Mum was at the end of her tether. It was confiscated but I managed to hold on to one of the drumsticks and was using it as a pretend sword as I marched up and down the lobby. At that precise moment, my grandad – on a visit to meet the church officer who was taking over from him – came in as I was behind the front door. It hit me and knocked me over, while the drumstick went straight up into my mouth, piercing my palate. My granny jumped to her feet when she heard my screams. 'Oh my,' was her exclamation for minor incidents, but this was an, 'Oh, mercy me!'

It was that serious.

Needless to say, grandad was full of remorse when he saw the blood pouring from my mouth. In fact, it was my own silly fault. I'll spare you the gory details but suffice to say that our GP, Dr Dunlop, realising it was an emergency, was on the scene very quickly. I ended up with stitches and a wire brace in my mouth. It must have been very painful, although after all this time I can't remember how painful. What bothered me most was that I would have to be fed with non-solid food and liquids for weeks not to mention having to 'calk ike hat' for as long as the contraption was inside my mouth. It would have been a challenge for any speech therapist, virtually unknown in those days, and even if they had been around, my parents wouldn't have been able to afford one.

It was around this time that I got to sleep with my first woman, and my own cousin at that. I know what you're thinking but get your dirty minds out of the gutter. It was actually my mother's idea. My parents were to attend the annual GEC dinner dance in the Grosvenor ballroom in Gordon Street, and, because they were going to be home late, I had to be decanted for the night. That meant Aunty Betty's house downstairs. That evening, young Betty, big Betty's eldest daughter, was getting ready to go out and dolling herself up at the dressing table, just along from the fireplace. She had pretentions to be a lady and would try to sound posh while Nana, her sister, a year younger than me, was a bit scatty.

'Now don't you dare go into that drawer,' Betty said to Nana. 'That's my hairbrush and I don't want you using it.' She knew Nana liked to play at hairdressers and would be in there like a shot when her back was turned. Which, of course, is exactly what happened. I was ushered into the chair as Nana's pretend customer. 'Short back and sides,' I confidently requested. Not a chance. This was a ladies' salon. Thank God she didn't have a perm in mind or we would have been there all night.

After my hairdressing appointment was over, aunty Betty quickly stepped in. 'Right you two, time for bed.' That meant a head-to-toe configuration, in case there was any hanky-panky. No fear. I was only nine and girls were still ugh. No, it was more 'stinky, stinky' and all above board, or should I say between sheets. After a few requests like, 'Move ower you,' swiftly followed by, 'No, move ower yersel,' sleep got the better of us.

A similar situation arose another night. This time it was down the road at the house of Nana's cousin. He was older than me and because I liked a model aeroplane he had built I had a certain admiration for him. But his mischievous side came out when we were in bed. He had sneaked some crinkly paper under the blankets and when we had settled down I heard a crackling sound and wondered what it could be. When he exclaimed, 'Quick, the hoose is on fire,' it sent me into a panic. I made such a din with my crying that his mother came through to see what was going on. When she discovered what he was up to, she gave him a good telling off and a 'skelpet leatherin' as well.

'Now get tae sleep,' were her last words on the matter as she left the room.

Tollcross park

One of the few amenities in the East End was Tollcross park. It had so many things to enjoy but my favourite was the museum. As you entered, the first animal you saw was Bob, a stuffed deer in a glass case facing the door. I felt, even at the tender age of six, that I knew him. That was because my mother always told me that she used to feed him when he was living in the park. I live in Ireland now and I met a lady from Tollcross who told me that her mother did the same thing; no doubt there are many similar stories out there.

Apart from the wonderful scale models of liners and battle-ships, the other museum exhibit that enthralled me was the story of 'Who killed Cock Robin?' He was behind a glass case, with the whole poem written alongside. 'I said the sparrow, with my bow and arrow,' and there was poor Cock Robin, lying on his back with an arrow in his chest, in a realistic pool of blood. Every bird and animal depicted in that glass case was real to me. Many a time I would stand there, marvelling at the story, wondering if I could somehow snap my fingers and make him come alive again. The Winter Gardens (otherwise known as the hothouse) too was a wonderful space. The smell was great and of course who could forget those big, bronze-coloured goldfish. At least they were alive. I think it may be appropriate, at this stage, to have a minute's silence for poor Cock Robin.

Then there were the entertainers who performed in that circular palace of songs, dance and mirth that was often referred to simply as 'the bandstand'. Someone from the departing act would be delegated to run back to announce the next act: 'And the next item on your programme is K 4,' as they flipped over the appropriate lettered and numbered slates on the stands at the corner of the stage. It was hoped this would match the number on the programme you were given when you paid the entrance charge, which was sixpence. It was about as sophisticated as things got in those days. Wilson Keppel and Betty, Doris Droy, Dave Willis, Sammy Murray; these were just a few of the names who trod the boards of the council's bandstands and who later became household names.

We had been playing in Tollcross park one summer's night when we witnessed a crowd of men gathering at the bottom of Wellshot Road. They were divided into two groups, with one man in each group the focus of attention. They weren't exactly hostile but they had a look of unfinished business about them. As they started to move off, two cops who had been standing at the police box across the road slowly began to keep pace with the groups, but keeping a respectable distance.

The two groups marched up Tollcross Road towards Causwayside Street, turning down past Victoria church and on to the spare ground beside the Masonic hall. It was apparent by now to the growing crowd, including us, that there was going to be a fight. The hostility may have been over a woman, or perhaps a difference of religion. Who knows. It was enough that we were there about to witness this pugilistic confrontation. You might be wondering why the men didn't go into Tollcross park and slug it out there. It was quite simple. The two officers belonged to the Glasgow police force, which meant that in order to avoid being arrested it was necessary for them to cross the city boundary and go into Lanarkshire. There was a good chance that the Lanarkshire constabulary wouldn't show up, hence the long walk.

The two main men removed their jackets and threw them to their respective pals, then squared up, fists at the ready. Tentative punches were thrown, trying to expose weaknesses in the opponent's defences. There were no gloves, stools, seconds, three-minute rounds or ropes but the strange thing was that no foul language was uttered by either of the two combatants, or even by the crowd. This was a serious contest and deserved the full concentration of all concerned. The only nasty sounds were the clashing of fists, the loosening of teeth and the crunching of faces as blow after blow landed.

In the beginning it could have passed for a professional bout, but, after about six or seven minutes, it was clear that tiredness had set in. Instead of bouncing around like pros, their movements were sluggish. They still threw the odd punch but with less weight behind each swing and their shirts were now well bloodied. The weaker of the two adversaries could take no more, hardly surprising given that both men were aged between 45 and 50. The supporters of the stronger man were happy that he'd got the better of his opponent, while the supporters on the other side had to restrain their man as he tried in vain to reach the winner with one last swing. But the main event was over.

It was still daylight, so we made our way to my grampa's ice-cream shop, hoping I could persuade him to let us have an oyster each. These were double wafers made in the shape of an oyster, with ice cream and raspberry inside, and they were one of his most sought-after delicacies. There were three of us and while my grampa wasn't mean, he had a business to run. 'Ah'll gie ye a pockey hat each, there ye are,' said he in his half-Scottish, half-Italian accent. Since we hadn't a penny between us, we had to settle for that and romped home quite happy.

Lloyd Avenue

Lloyd Avenue was where my cousin Jim lived. His father, my uncle Willie, worked in Stewarts & Lloyds just across the field at the back of their house. I think they only paid part rent, with the balance being met by the steelworks, and for obvious reasons the houses were called the 'steel houses'. The family, Willie, his wife Eva and their only son Jim, lived upstairs while their neighbours lived below them. They had a two-room-and-kitchen and a bathroom just off the kitchen. That was luxury!

I loved to go their house to play, because there was so much to play with. Uncle Willie had been in the First World War and he had brought back a British helmet, a German helmet and a real bayonet. As you can imagine how that led to all sorts of games, although Jim had been warned not to remove the bayonet from its sheath, which was kept hidden away just in case. The British helmet had leather padding but the German helmet was a beauty: it was black and had a brass spike sticking out the top, with a large gold eagle on the front; that was the one I fancied but Jim, being older than me, had first choice.

The Second World War had started by now and everybody knew what Hitler looked like because Charlie Chaplin did a much-copied impression of him in his 1940 film, *The Great Dictator*. Jim would parody him by putting his left forefinger under his nose, shooting his right arm out, clicking his heels and shouting, 'Heil Hitler'. That gave him a certain superiority and a great deal of satisfaction into the bargain. The games would go on and soon it was my turn for the helmet; I would launch into the same trick because everything Jim did, I would do too. He was my hero.

When the weather was good we would play in the garden. Jim had a great train set, with rails, a signal box, trucks, signals and buffers; I could go on and on, I was besotted. The engine was called *The Duke of York*, wheel configuration of 4/4; you must know what that means by now. This engine pulled a coal tender that could be unhooked. However, he had the knack of lifting and laying both of them together, on and off the track, using one hand. Therefore, I had the impression the tender was attached. Some days we would go into the field and fly our model aeroplanes. Cousin Jim's planes always had a propeller, which made them fly for ever without crashing, while mine was a simple, cheap glider that invariably fell to earth not long after it was launched.

On rainy days we would play inside. He had a game, Buccaneer, which consisted of a large board on which pirate ships were moved around between islands. I was right there on that ship, becoming a pirate for a good hour. Like me, Jim was great at drawing and we would play a quiz of our own making, in which one of us would draw a small part of an aeroplane and the other would have to guess the plane it belonged to. Even though I was younger than him, I always managed to win, probably because I was an avid reader of *The Aeroplane Spotter,* a newspaper-type magazine produced during the war for us mad enthusiasts.

Jim had a big, open-out book of plans of Second World War aeroplanes, from which he built his models. I watched in awe as he crafted them out of balsa wood. Even when Skybird brought out their range of aeroplane kits, they were just lumps of wood that had to be sanded into shape, and that was too much for me. My time was to come, years later, when the Airfix range of plastic models was introduced and all I had to do was glue the ready-shaped parts together and apply the camouflage. That was more like it.

In the late afternoon, the evening papers would be delivered to aunt May's newsagent's shop in Clarkston Road. My mother often helped out, as the bundles containing the *Citizen* and the *Evening Times* were flung through the door and had to be sorted and laid out on the counter for customers on the way home from work. I was able to get my weekly copy of the *The Aeroplane Spotter* there, which I devoured from cover to cover. One afternoon, me and my pals were playing on Cemetery Road, the road that leads from the gates to Cathcart cemetery. During one of our games I had run across to the other side of the main road and it was then I saw a German bomber over the north of the city. There happened to be a man in RAF uniform standing at the car stop and I thought I had better warn him, reasoning that he would be able to do something.

'Look, there's a Heinkel 111 away over there,' I shouted.

He looked at me as if I had two heads and calmly replied, 'Oh aye. Is that right son?'

The poor fella was home on leave and the last thing he wanted was to be reminded of the war, especially by a daft wee boy. I ran off, feeling slighted by his attitude, but I had no sooner run into the shop when the sirens went off. I glanced back at him and wished I could have shouted over, 'See, I told you so.' The lone bomber was either shot down or chased back to Germany as nothing seemed to be happening and no one was in a panic.

Meanwhile, a nephew of my grannie, Rankin Muir, of the A. & R. Muir dynasty of sculptors, happened to be in the shop, and on learning that I was Jean Lightbody's son, flashed his wallet and asked me, 'Well Walter what would you like? You can choose anything you want.' Aunt May's shop didn't stock aeroplane kits or anything that exciting. Being surprised by this act of generosity, and after some hasty deliberations, I opted for a silly little, white, wooden rowing boat. That was it. Rankin had made his gesture, and, pleased that I hadn't thrown him into debt at the bank, stuffed his wallet back into his inside jacket pocket and was told the price, which was sixpence. He handed it over the counter with a gratuitous smile. Knowing what I know now, aunt May should have charged him a couple of quid for the damn thing.

Going home much later we caught the no. 5 car coming from Kirklee into town and changed onto the 29 travelling east to Tollcross. It was dark and the lights were on inside the car, dim blue lights behind small tin shades because of the blackout. 'Fares please,' the conductor shouted as he came along the car. With great difficulty, my mother fished out the tuppence for her and a ha'ppeny for me from her purse. The conductor clicked his machine and I got to hold the tickets. Being a restless little bugger, I was on my knees looking over the back of the seat, when a drunk man got on and sat down. He was facing me, with his eyes half closed due to the amount of drink consumed.

I loved to watch drunks, so long as they were happy, and this man fitted the bill. He kept trying to look out of the window, but would quickly give up, despite wiping the steam on the window with his sleeve. He was muttering something and giving me the occasional smile. My mother, recognising this, pulled me round to face frontwards but I was determined to watch his laboured movements and the swaying from side to side. We were long past Bellgrove and coming up to Camlachie when the conductor bent over and asked the man where he wanted to get off. 'Porkheid Cross,' he drawled. Before the conductor turned away my new friend gave him a more precise instruction: 'the Straw Hoose,' he shouted, after bringing the words to mind.

I call him my friend because I was with him in spirit, if you'll excuse the pun.

Holidays

During the years between moving to Tollcross and the beginning of the war there was so much going on in my life, I was enjoying Wellshot school and doing well there. There were holidays too. My father worked in the GEC and he always took his holidays during the last fortnight in August. I don't remember much about the camping holiday at Ayr and I don't think my mother enjoyed it as much as he did, him being a frustrated boy scout perhaps. As long as I had my pail and spade I was happy.

The holidays I loved, because I was older and could appreciate them more, were the ones we spent just outside Stanley, which is seven miles north of Perth. They wouldn't have cost my father a lot as we stayed with his aunt Annie, a sister of Gran Bernardini. The hamper was packed and off we went to a house called Leeside cottage. It had no running water and thank goodness it wasn't raining when we were there as we had to wash in the basin outside. This was country life, something we weren't used to in Glasgow. I got to feed the hens, which was a new experience. She also had two pigs and there was something about them I loved; they couldn't keep me away. I loved their grunting and of course I would grunt back, which I got quite good at by the time we left.

Another sister of my gran lived on a farm, a real farm where me and my mum got to help with bringing in the hay. To get to the farm you had to cross the main railway line and it was there that I watched from a safe distance as the next express train came thundering past on its way to Inverness or Aberdeen. When all was quiet, I rested my ear on the rail and I could hear the sound of oncoming trains while they were miles off. There was forest on either side of the track as far as the eye could see and that, together with the smell of the pines and the total silence except for some bird call, made the whole experience magical.

The next holiday was in 1939. We went to the Isle of Man, which today would have been like going to Majorca. It was my father's usual last two weeks in August, which meant that we were only home for a week before war was declared. At Ardrossan we boarded the I.O.M. Steam Packet Co. ship, *Tynwald*. Interestingly, in the newsreel footage showing the evacuation of Dunkirk, the ship you can see in the background is either the *Tynwald*, or her sister ship *The King Orry*. By that time, they had been pressed into war service and were painted battleship grey. We had a beautiful day for our sail to Douglas. One of my fondest memories was the song being sung by passengers as we sat on the coiled ropes at the back of the ship under a scorching sun, a popular number called 'South of the Border Down Mexico Way'.

While we were there, we went on a day cruise to Llandudno on a lovely white ship with an orange funnel, the *St Seiriol*. During the voyage we saw the stern of something peculiar sticking out of the water as we neared Llandudno. Although we weren't aware of it at the time, this turned out to be the stern of HMS *Thetis*, which had sunk on sea trials with the loss of ninety-nine lives. When we got back, with the threat of war looming, my mother began to think of my safety and that of course meant evacuation.

Wartime

Evacuation

In the early days of 1940, with the war in full swing, my mother worried about my safety. Evacuation was the obvious answer, but where to? I wasn't one of those children you may have seen on telly, lined up in a queue, waiting for transport to faraway places, gas masks in square cardboard boxes round their necks. Mum had an aunt, Jean, who lived in Carluke, and although it was only twenty-five miles up the road from Tollcross, she reckoned it would be far enough away. She also had the comfort of knowing that I would be in safe hands and well looked after by a close relative. I was also familiar with Aunt Jean, because we would sometimes go up to visit her and her husband Jim on a Sunday. So that was where I was being sent, although given the choice, I would have much preferred Largs, simply because it had a boating pond. But Carluke it was, like it or lump it.

Aunt Jean was very nice. Strict, but nice. Uncle Jim, on the other hand, seemed strange. He suffered from consumption and would sit all day long in his chair, coughing and spluttering into a spittoon by his feet. That took a bit of getting used to. Their address was 21 Cassell's Street, although the main entrance was from the rear, past a ground-floor, two-storey house and into a yard. An outside stone stairway led up to their door, and beneath the stair there was the outside toilet. When you went into the house, it felt cosy and smelt of polished wood. It was lit by gas, which at night would fascinate me with its occasional pop, while the glow from the mantle would leave the corners of the room dark and mysterious.

I had a new companion: Brian, their lovely Irish setter. I had seen him many times on previous visits but he now became my best friend. Brian had been a show dog and his full title was Brian Bournville, followed by two dog-show titles, which don't come readily to mind. He was my uncle Jim's pride and joy and had won prizes at shows all over the country. There was a beautiful painting of him, standing side on, head up and tail straight out, which hung proudly on their wall. It had been painted by my granny's brother, Tom Paterson, a regular exhibitor in Glasgow's fine-art exhibitions. I have two watercolours of his, but I don't know what became of the painting of Brian, which I would dearly love to have hanging on my wall today.

There was a long, narrow corridor that ran the full length of the house, down to the room where I slept. The room was at the front of the house, overlooking the main street, and could be noisy, especially at weekends. It was now Monday morning, my first day at the new school, and, excited about what lay ahead, I woke early. I heard Brian padding along the narrow lobby, his tail slapping off the walls. I felt his cold, wet nose in between the blankets, urging me to get up. He was such a clever dog; I wouldn't have been surprised if he knew it was my first day at school and was every bit as excited as I was.

Aunt Jean's porridge and a piece-and-marmalade inside me and we were off. My schoolbag was light as it contained only a pencil case with freshly sharpened pencils and a rubber, as well as a wee piece for lunch. We didn't have far to walk to the school, and, as we entered, you could have cut the atmosphere with a knife. 'Oh, oh . . . a stranger in town.' I was shown where to sit and as I waved goodbye to aunt Jean I was on my own. I can't remember what went on during lessons, except that it was very much like Wellshot school back in Tollcross. The teacher was very nice, and my fellow pupils, boys and girls, were all very attentive, as I was. It was when the bell rang for playtime that the difference between our worlds became apparent. We stood there in silence, eyeing each other up and down.

It was the biggest boy who spoke first.

'You're a wee Glesca keely, urn't ye?' This was followed by a few 'ayes' from the others.

It was the first time I had heard the expression, 'Glesca keely', but if that's what I was, so be it, because I was in no position to argue. The next day, I was brave enough to draw their attention to my secret weapons – my tackety boots! I was the only boy with such upmarket gear, coming as I did from the sophisticated big city. They weren't weapons of war, they were for sliding; think of them as the 1940s equivalent of the skateboard. Like all my pals in Tollcross, they were an essential part of winter wear and if you didn't own a pair you were a nobody. I had at least twenty tackets, or segs, on each sole and eight on the heels, and I don't think they had heard of such essential additions in rural Lanarkshire. I'm sure the Carluke cobblers must have thought Christmas had come early because the mothers of my new classmates were at their doors asking: 'Can you cover the soles an' heels o' ma boy's boots wi' thae segs the same as the wee Glesca keely has? As many as ye can get on each bit.'

From then on, I was in with the 'in crowd'. This wee Glesca keely was one of them now, so I had to get used to referring to my boots as 'bits'.

On Saturday mornings I would go to the Windsor, the picture house that overlooked the square at the top of the town. There I would watch the latest weekly cowboy serials. To start with, Tom Mix was the main attraction, but he wasn't as good as Hopalong Cassidy and his horse Topper, who took over and thrilled us to bits with his silver six-shooters. I'd sit there excitedly munching an apple down to the core, then stride out into the daylight, jump on my horse and gallop back down the main street, left arm gripping the reins while my right-hand slapped Topper's backside, (well mine actually). No doubt, the locals would be saying, 'There goes that mad Glesca keely wi' his tackety bits slappin' his erse as if it was a horse.' Well it was!

Once I had ridden through the close and tied Topper to the railings, I would run up the stairs for my dinner. I could smell those oniony tatties a mile away. Mmm! A clap for Brian who was waiting for me at the top of the stairs and straight into the house. As soon as I got in, there would be immediate instructions from my aunt.

'Wash yer hands.'

'Ah know.'

After my hands had been inspected I would be served sliced sausage, the Saturday speciality. After a great morning at the pictures it fitted the bill perfectly.

After my dinner, I would make my way over too see my new girlfriend, Ena Thomson. I thought she was my girlfriend, but it was more adoration for the big sister I never had. Ena lived in the two-storey house at the entrance to the yard I mentioned previously. She must have been three or four years older than me but I was besotted with her; I even had a child-hood vision of marrying her someday. So, there I was, chapping at the door despite aunt Jean warning me not to be a nuisance.

'Hello Mrs Thomson. Is Ena in?'

'Oh aye, come on in son'.

She could have been hiding somewhere, but no, there she was, sitting at the table.

'Oh, hello Walter.' She had spoken to me and that was enough to set my pulse racing.

'Dae ye want tae come oot tae play?' I asked, in my best Carluke accent.

What a stupid question.

'No, ave tae feenish ma homework.'

She was at the big school and they got homework to do. Undaunted I asked, 'Can a watch ye?' just so that I could look into her eyes for a bit longer.

'No' the noo son. She has tae concentrate,' her mother inter-rupted, 'cos she's got an exam comin' up.'

I could take a hint, even at that age.

'Okay then. Cheerio Mrs Thomson.'

'Cheerio son. Ye'll maybe see her the morn.'

'Cheerio Ena,' I shouted as I went out the door, but her head was buried in her books. Never mind, maybe next time.

I spent a lot of time at the square. There I would breathe in the heavenly aroma of jam and tobacco; a strange mixture, but let me explain. Scott's jam factory wasn't far down the road, and the smell of strawberry jam, mingled with the smoke coming from the old men's pipes as they sat on the benches in the square, was my fix for the day. Thick Black and Erinmore were the two most pungent varieties of tobaccos and they filled the air. Erinmore was the smell I loved best because that was what my father smoked and it reminded me of him and, naturally enough, home. My mother and father would come up every so often at the weekend and I would get to enjoy the smell from his pipe. Sometimes my granny and grandad Lightbody came with them. My grandad was born in Carluke, and had played football for them in his youth, so it was like going back home. Of course, I also looked forward to any wee treats they brought with them.

All too soon, aunt Jean, myself and Brian, would be walking them up to the cross to say goodbye till the next visit. While waiting for the 241 bus, which came all the way from Lanark, I would often look across at the war memorial, surrounded by its white stone pillars and sagging black steel chains with an eight-pointed star at the centre of each. 'Their name liveth for ever-more' was the standard wording, together with the names of the local men who gave their lives in the 1914–18 war. The 'Great War' they called it; I used to wonder what was great about it. Would the war that was on at that time – the cause of my temporary displacement – be called, the 'Great, Great War' or perhaps the 'Really Great War'? My reverie was interrupted by the sound of the familiar red single-decker 241 bus. It was time to say goodbye with a kiss, a wee tear from my mother and a 'You be a good boy now, d'ye hear?' from my father.

It was time for us to walk back in the gathering dusk, to the comforting flicker of the gas lamp and the shadows on the wall, then off to bed.

My mother brought me a torch on one of her visits. She thought it would be useful for going up and down the stairs to the outside lavatory at aunt Jean's. The torch had a two-way switch, one for a normal 'see-your-way-in-the-dark' light for shining on to the ground, the other for switching to a fantastic, long-range beam. Why it had that facility in those times, I'll never know, but it was the Devil's own temptation for a carefree boy of eight.

We would take Brian up past a place called the Cairnamount, where aunt Jean had a relation. After the visit – I was always given a wee biscuit – we made our way to the vacant ground farther up so that Brian would be able to run free and sniff at anything that took his fancy. One night it got dark early and as we walked across the field, I was shining my new torch on the ground in the proper manner. But all the while, I could hear a voice in my ear urging, 'go on I dare you'. I could resist no longer, so while aunt Jean was preoccupied with checking on Brian's whereabouts, and it had got really dark, I thought, 'this is it'. I switched to full beam and shone the torch upwards to see if it would reach the sky. It did.

I discovered immediately that I had done something bad.

'Pit that light oot.'

It was a woman's voice, not the regular ARP warden. Aunt Jean swung round, as quick as a flash – if you'll excuse the pun – and whipped the torch from my grasp.

'Don't ever do that again,' she said, in a sterner tone than she'd ever used with me before. It was probably for the benefit of the woman who had shouted and who was now by our side, her dog and Brian sniffing each other like doggie friends do.

'Oh, it's you Aggie. A thocht a recognised your voice.'

'Aye, it's me awright.'

They were obviously friends, as Aggie lived next door to her relation in the Cairnamount.

'Now yer no tae be daen that again son. Ye micht hiv brocht wan o' they German aeroplanes ower tae drap a bomb on us,' said Aggie, albeit in a less severe tone.

What German aeroplane would be interested in dropping a bomb on Carluke? It only had a jam factory and the Germans had more strategic targets to consider.

'Guid nicht Aggie,' as we reached her house.

'Guid nicht then Jean. Will ye see yer wey doon the road?'

'Och aye, we've got Walter's torch, haven't we, ya wee devil?' addressing her remark both to Aggie and to me, this time with a friendly nudge.

Sometimes, we would take Brian for a long walk to the North British railway station, which was about halfway to Wishaw. The disused station had been turned into a large area where aeroplanes damaged in battle were brought as scrappage or repair. Aunt Jean knew that I loved it there as it allowed me to get close to the machines that played such a great part in my imagination. I would always be lying on the floor drawing aeroplanes in battle, with soundtrack to match. I could never draw aeroplanes without mimicking the 'weeeows' and 'rat-tat-tats' of the machine guns that the drawings demanded. Well, here they were in real life, right in front of me.

Although some were very badly damaged, I could still test my recognition skills and was in awe of the sight that greeted me.

'Oh look, there's an Avro Anson; there's a Lysander and that's a Messerschmitt 110,' I would say to myself. My favourite bomber at the time was the Vickers Wellington, and sure enough there was one there that day. I knew it had been designed by Barnes Wallis, who was to become famous for the invention of the 'bouncing bomb' used in the famous Dambusters raid later in the war. Although the Wellington was badly damaged, through the torn outer fabric I could see the geodesic criss-cross wooden structure, which, because of its light weight, gave the plane its great manoeuvrability and speed. This one had taken a real pounding but fortunately had made it home.

Aunt Jean must have been bored (as indeed some of you ladies must be with all his technical information). Of course, she was caring enough to leave me engrossed while she took Brian farther round the field and when she came back to collect me it was time to go home for tea. It never seemed to rain in those days and we both enjoyed the long walk. I was allowed to hold Brian's lead because he was tired and she knew he wouldn't pull me off my feet; anyway, I could always slide with my tackety boots. Downhill from the cross it was easier and we were soon back, having bought something for tea on the way.

It was coming to the middle of August and the weather was still good. The tackety boots were long gone and I was now wearing my sandshoes, or, to put it into Glesga slang, 'sawnies'. No good for sliding, but great for running fast.

I loved trains as well as planes, in fact anything mechanical if it was painted in nice colours and moved majestically, whether on land, sea or in the air. It was time to go down to the station to watch the express, which I knew would be coming soon. I hoped it would be pulled by one of the big engines, either the Duchess class, or, if I was lucky, one of the new, streamlined Coronation class on the LMS line. I wouldn't be able to see the famous record-breaking *Flying Scotsman* because it was on the LNER route from Edinburgh to London.

I got to the station in plenty of time. There was no one else there apart from the stationmaster, Mr McAlpine, who was busy sweeping the platform with a huge broom. I knew his name because he had made himself known to us, in no uncertain terms, when me and some other lads were messing about and he checked us. He repeated his warning from that first encounter.

'Keep well back son. Don't go too near the edge.'

'Yes Mr McAlpine,' I shouted, 'I will,' in a suitably deferential tone, careful to keep on his good side this time.

It was eerily quiet, except for the sound of birds chirping and the noise of his brush sweeping the platform. No sign of the train though.

Let me introduce you to musical sounds associated with steam trains and the rails. Years ago, rails were laid in sections and, between them, there was a gap of a couple of inches to allow for expansion in hot weather. This is where the musical sounds come in. There were three types of sounds made by the wheels as they crossed the gaps. A goods train, being slow, would go, 'dumdum dumdum … dumdum dumdum … dumdum dumdum,' while the faster local trains would go 'didldidum … didldidum … didldidum … didldidum'. An express train, being really fast, would sound like, 'diddlydee diddlydum …

diddlydee diddlydum . . . diddlydee diddlydum' and when the last carriage had finally crossed over the gap in the rails, you would hear 'didum didum didum' fading away into the distance. Remember to keep your tongue striking the back of your teeth as fast as you can. I know you're doing it. Go on, admit it.

Oh, here it comes. I can just make out the shape away in the distance now. I know it's one of the '4, 6, 2' probably the *Duchess of Atholl*. Those numbers relate to the wheel arrangements: four wee wheels (called bogies), at the front, two on each side, three driving wheels on each side and two bogies behind. Whoosh, it's passing me now, too fast to read the name on the side of the engine – 'diddlydee diddlydum . . . diddlydee diddlydum' and on and on until that last 'didum didum didum'. As the noise faded, it left only me, the stationmaster and the birds breaking the silence. Then it was back up the road for tea.

I hope you enjoyed that wee hurl.

My time at Carluke was coming to an end. I had been away for ten months and given that the Dunkirk evacuation had been such a success perhaps it was also time to bring me home. I had no argument with that, and while I had enjoyed many aspects of my experience, I was glad that my parents had come to that decision.

On the day my mother and father came to collect me, it was raining. This added to the sombre atmosphere. I was parting from an aunt I had grown to like, and an uncle who had accepted my young presence without complaint. I had come to love many things about Carluke: the NB station with its discarded aircraft; the lingering smell of jam and tobacco at the cross; the speeding express trains; the magic daylight in the hallway and the ghostly glimmer of the gas lamp at night; those oniony potatoes; my best pal Brian, whom I would miss most of all. I forgot to mention Ena, but she was too grown up to bother with me at that time.

Aunt Jean insisted she would come with us to the cross despite the dreich day, as Brian needed the walk. I was glad because I would be able to hold him by the lead for one last time. The parting was sad, but as it turned out we were to visit Carluke a few times after that, mostly on sad occasions. Uncle Jim died but I wasn't there for his funeral. I can't help wondering if they buried his spittoon along with him. Aunt Jean and Brian were still there and I saw them again on subsequent visits.

I clearly remember one time we were on our way home, together with my granny. It was getting dark and we were seated at the front of the bus. Bored, I was looking for something to do to break the tedium. I was standing facing the back of the bus and kept watching the conductor. So, I thought, I'll press the big metal stud on the division between the driver and the passengers at the same time as he pressed the bell at the back of the bus to let people on and off. I was having a great time and enjoying the smiles of the woman behind me, who knew what I was up to. My granny, however, who had been watching, turned to my mother and said: 'Oh my, Jean, stoap him daein' that or the conductor'll be up tae gie him intae a row.' My mother realised what was going on and I was immediately given a strict order: 'Stop your nonsense,' I was instructed. That put an end to my wee game.

On much later visits to Carluke, things had changed a great deal. The Americans were in town. Vera Lynn's rendition of

'The White Cliffs of Dover', which could be heard coming from radios during my evacuation, was being replaced by such as 'From the Halls of Montezuma to the Shores of Tripoli' – a line from the anthem of the US Marine Corps – and 'Boogie-Woogie Bugle Boy'. The presence of the Yanks was tangible, helped by the number of Jeeps buzzing around and the large Chevys and Buicks painted in drab green with white stars on the side to ferry the officers around.

Poor Brian had gone by that time and aunt Jean wasn't in the best of health. One of her final acts before she died was to take my mother up to Lennoxtown to clear out the attic where my granny's artist brother, Tom Paterson, had spent his last days. He had become a slave to alcohol and gave away paintings for the price of a drink. Such a shame considering that he could have been one of the most heralded names on the Scottish art scene. As a result of the house clearance, I became the beneficiary of a number of his brushes, paints and a beautiful large wooden palette, which I use to this day. I have two of his best paintings, which I had grown up with in Shettleston and in our house in Tollcross.

I want to mention a wee memory here. The name 'Aunt Polly' would come up in conversation from time to time. She was my granny's sister and had emigrated to New Zealand a long time ago. The only link with her was a magazine that we would occasionally receive in the post, containing beautiful pictures of snow-covered mountains and lakes from that far-off land. Aunt Polly continued to be a name from the past until one day in 2011 I received an email from a lady in New Zealand called Rosalie Purchase. The name meant nothing to me but her email contained the signature 'T. Paterson' at the foot of one of the pictures in her possession. Rosalie asked if I recognised it. I did. So, I immediately photographed the matching signature on one of our paintings and sent it to her.

'Hi cousin,' came the reply.

It turned out that Rosalie is a single lady and devoted to travelling. We developed a strong bond through email and she later cemented our relationship by visiting us in Ireland on one of her many tours. Rosalie, I discovered, is the granddaughter of the mysterious aunt Polly, whose name wasn't Polly at all, but, in fact, Mary. We imagine Polly must have been a nickname from her youth, and now, thanks to the internet, the long-lost mysteries of both uncle Tom and aunt Polly were revealed.

I had gained another relative.

Home from Carluke

Back at 1060, I was well and truly back home, albeit to a changed close from the one I had left ten months ago. A baffle wall had been erected on the pavement outside the close and wooden scaffolding installed all along the inside and up over the roof, giving it a cathedral-like effect. It had been put there to strengthen the plaster walls, but we were happy to use it to climb up there and hide, making scary noises as people passed underneath.

As time went by, I grew accustomed to being three stairs up. At certain times of the year you could see the Northern Lights out of the front room where I slept. If you lifted the window right up, and leaned out far enough, you could see Tinto hill away to the south. Of course, at my age, it didn't mean much; it could have been Mount Etna for all I knew. For the first time too, I was meeting up with my relations. These were my cousins: Nana, who lived on the first landing below us, while May and David Bernardini stayed in Corbett Street. They spent more time over at my gran and grampa's ice-cream shop because their mother and father, James and Nora, were at work all day.

I only had one cousin on the Lightbody side of the family. That was Jim, who was older than me, and my hero because he could make model aeroplanes and battleships out of balsa wood. I remained friends with Eddie Mitchell, he of the through-the-wall-rail-link story. Eddie's folks moved from 592 Shettleston Road to Denbrae Street because he had two big sisters and two big brothers and they needed more room. It was easy for me to keep in touch as it wasn't far along Wellshot Road. I looked forward to our visits to the Mitchells, as Eddie and I enjoyed playing together.

Another three playmates at Tollcross were Elspeth and Morag Blair, who lived below us, and May Keating, who lived up the next close. If I wasn't doing anything, I was roped in to play the husband in their family games on the stairs, especially on wet days. I had to accept my role as I was outnumbered on the gender side. During the game, I would be made to drink imaginary tea out of cups from their tea sets. 'One spoonful please,' and all that carry on. I also got steak and chips if I had just got home from work. I played along with their domestic fantasy and I would still be starving at the end of it all.

We had a light show every night in half-hour intervals; it came from the Clyde Ironworks. Its source was the slag heap, an ever-increasing mound of earth with a rail track on top. A wee engine would chug its way up, shoving a truck load of slag (hot, molten, unwanted steel), and dump it over the end. The burning metal sent a red-hot glow up into the sky, which would die down gradually. The whole operation lasted about ten minutes, during which time we would be treated to a weird, almost addictive, fireworks display. No wonder it was called Dixon's Blazes.

It came to an abrupt end. Not only was there an eclipse of the moon, on a Friday the thirteenth, but also the Germans took this opportunity to see their way clearly to Clydebank in 1941.

The Blitz

I had been brought home from Carluke after ten months of evacuation, as both my mother and father thought that the air raids had passed. How wrong they were.

It was close to nine at night on 13 March 1941. My mother had just washed her hair and was drying it when the air-raid sirens sounded. I was to be given a dose of castor oil and I wasn't looking forward to it. I had been standing at the long wooden counter adjoining the sink, turning the dreaded bottle over from left to right, watching the heavy liquid as it rolled back and forth, pondering what was to come. My father was a sub officer in the Auxiliary Fire Service, (the AFS) and that night he was on duty at Wellshot where the Auxiliary fire engine was parked.

'Quick get yer warm coat on,' my mother shouted. That meant we were going down into the close. For anyone who isn't familiar with the word *close*, it's the name given to the entrance from the street, and runs through to the back court. Stone stairs led up to the third floor and housed three families on each landing. The close was to be our shelter for as long as the raid lasted.

Chairs were brought down and everyone huddled together with blankets brought down from the house, as there was always a draught blowing through from both ends of the close despite the baffle wall that had been erected at the entrance during my absence. (Baffle walls were rectangular structures made of corrugated iron and filled with sand to deflect bomb blasts.)

At first, we were all cheery, trying to make the best of things. Ten o'clock came and went . . . then eleven o'clock and still no all-clear. It looked as if we were in for a long night. 'Wheesht,' cried Mrs Neilson, who lived one stair up, as the drone, drone, drone of the German bombers got louder and louder. During the war, I was able to recognise almost any aeroplane, their speed, wingspan, the make of their engines and the sound each one made. There's a good reason I was so knowledgeable; I was a mad keen reader of *The Aeroplane Spotter*, a weekly paper published for us young followers of the air war.

I was enjoying this new experience. 'I bet they're Dornier 17s by the sound of their Mercedes Benz engines,' I would be thinking to myself.

'Wheesht,' this time from Mrs Todd, who lived on the second floor, below us. I never liked her. She was always checking us for something or other, grumpy old bitch.

Bang! Right outside the close this time.

'Is that a bomb?' Mrs Blair asked. She was a nice woman, who lived across from Mrs Todd. She had two daughters, Elspeth, whom I used to play with, and Morag a bit younger. I knew it wouldn't be a bomb; we would have been blown to kingdom come if it had been. No, it was one of the mobile anti-aircraft guns mounted on the backs of trucks that ran up and down the road. Fat lot of good they did; they kept firing into the night sky at targets they couldn't even see, trying to convince the public that they would eventually hit something. 'We'll get ye the,' guns were saying, but the Germans had business to attend to and they knew it.

'Ah'll need tae go tae the bathroom,' I heard someone say.

'Aye, so will I,' from another voice, further along the close.

Bathroom! That's a laugh. The 'cludgie' on the first landing more like, and it got well used that night. It was one in the morning now and we were into a new day. 'Oh great, that means there'll be no school tomorrow,' I thought. (When an air raid went on after eleven o' clock, you didn't have to go to school the next day.)

Another thud. 'My God that wis close,' shouted Mrs Ingram, who lived opposite us. At that moment, Tommy Ingram decided to take his life in his hands by going out round the back. 'Come back in here, ye'll get yersel' killed,' Mrs Ingram roared. Tommy shouted that he could see a parachute floating over Colville's steelworks. Of course, yours truly knew it was most likely a landmine. These devices were too big to be housed in the bomb racks; they were attached to parachutes and would float down to their intended target and cause an almighty explosion, far greater than any bomb. Tommy could see it clearly because there was an eclipse of the moon, precisely why the Germans chose that night to carry out such a concentrated raid. He wasn't long back inside the close when the whole building shook. I was right, it was a landmine. Another wee tick for my wartime knowledge.

The next wave of bombers droned overhead. Heinkel 111s by the sound of them. They had a familiar 'rumm, rumm, rumm', which was easy to recognise. Mr Neilson, from one stair up, remarked 'Will they never stoap comin'? Ye'd think they wid have run oot o' petrol be noo.'

'Ye mean diesel Mr Neilson. Remember they're German,' I said under my breath, out of respect for the elderly.

Just then, Nana, my cousin who lived two stairs down from us, whispered to her mother, 'Mammy I am needin',' her mammy being my auntie Betty. We had many Bettys in the Bernardini family. There was Big Betty, that was her, then we had 'oor' Betty, her eldest, and she was quite the lady among them all. Young Betty was next; she was my uncle Gordon's daughter from Parkhead. Then there was Betty from Troon; she was my father's auntie Maisie's daughter. I am sorry for going on a bit, but I'm only trying to acquaint you with all the Bettys with the name Bernardini.

'Who's got the lavvy key?' Big Betty enquired. The toilet on the first landing was in constant use that night because it was only half a stair up. They were all scared to go up to the next landing in case a bomb struck the building. That's a laugh because if there had been a direct hit, it wouldn't have mattered which landing you were on.

It must have been catching because it was my turn next. My mother took me up, and when I was in there she asked, impatiently, 'Are ye no finished yet?' I wasn't finished. I had opened the lavatory window, not to let the smell out, but because I wanted to see if Colville's was still there. I forgot I was only one stair up, so all I could see was the washhouse, the Central church and a few headstones in the graveyard over the wall. Anyway, we got safely back down to the close, together with the lavvy key, which was still much in demand. We re-joined our neighbours, most of whom were trying to get a wee sleep in between the now distant rumblings.

We could still hear stragglers on their way back to Germany after their deadly work. My cousin Nana and I started playing a wee game of guess-the-film-stars-by-their-initials'.

'Okay, you go first,' she said.

'No, you go first.'

'Okay. BD.'

'Umm, Bette Davis.'

'Och that wis easy.'

Nana next. 'RC.'

A wee bit harder.

'Oh, ah've got it. Ronald Coleman.'

We played on until we got fed up.

'Ah'm no playin' any more,' Nana sighed.

'Awright then,' I agreed.

It must have been getting late, or should I say early, as things had been quiet for a while. It was coming up to five in the morning on the fourteenth and we were still stuck in the close, having been there since nine the night before. Everybody was tired and fed up. 'Whit aboot a wee song?' says Mrs Neilson. 'Oh awright,' said her man. And with that he started to sing. 'Merzidoats an' dozydoats an' littlelamsetivy an' akittlytivytoo. Wouldn't you?'

'That's a stupid sang,' said Lizzie, who was from the middle door on the first landing.

'A thought it might cheer youse up,' Mr Neilson explained.

I must break into the story at this point to tell you that since I first heard it away back then, I thought it the silliest song with the most meaningless lyrics. However, hearing it many years later, as it was being aired on some nostalgic radio programme, it finally dawned on me what the words really meant. 'Mares eat oats and does eat oats and little lambs eat ivy. A kid'll eat ivy too – wouldn't you?' Still a silly song. Now back to the close.

'Okay. I'll sing ye another nice wan,' said Mr Ingram. 'There's a long, long trail a winding, into the land of my dreams.'

This one I knew; it was one my father had taught me and I had learned to harmonise to it. 'That was very nice son,' said Mrs Ingram who must have been listening through her dozing. The song went on, 'where the nightingales are singing in the wooooooo . . .'

Another great 'wheesht', this time from auntie Betty.

'That sounds like the all clear,' someone said.

'Yer right. It's aboot time tae,' Mrs Blair agreed.

'Thank God fur that. Ma legs are as stiff as pokers. D'ye think they'll be back? They must be goin' hame fur their tea, by this time. Even thae Jerries huv tae eat,' Mrs Rooney remarked. I never said a word!

Then there was another observation from aunt Betty. 'That wis a long time we've been doon here. Come on Nana, upstairs tae bed.' Another voice piped up as she folded up her blanket, 'See that bloody Hitler. If a could only get ma hauns on him ah'd wring his bloody neck.' And believe me she would have, given half a chance. For once I had to agree with her. Look out Mr Schicklgruber, Mrs Todd's after you.

When everyone had gathered their belongings and were making their way upstairs, a few of us tried to see what all the bombing was about. A red glow in the sky away over Glasgow to the west made it clear that it had taken place down by the docks. It turned out to be the infamous Clydebank raid.

'Right ma lad. That's enough excitement for one night.'

'But a don't want tae go tae bed. Ah'm no tired.'

'No tired! Ye need a couple o' matches to keep yer eyes open. C'mon, get up them sters, honey pers.'

Even at that time in the morning my mother could quote a popular Glasgow phrase of the time. I heard someone else saying, 'A wonder if Stirlin's is working.'

'Don't be daft,' says Isa, middle door, two stairs up. 'They'd be mad tae be bakin' wi' a' this goin' on.'

Stirling's was the bakers just up from our close with a shop on Tollcross Road and a bakery at the back, off the avenue leading to Central church. Sure enough, they had been baking all night, God bless them, because it meant everybody was able to buy their newly baked hot rolls that morning.

My mother opened the door to the house we had left in a hurry nine hours before, and guess what was still there beside the sink? Aye, the dreaded castor-oil bottle, its contents now settled in a menacing glug at the bottom. Remembering what we'd just been through, or rather what had been through us during the night, I hoped it would be classed as redundant at that stage and put back on the shelf where it belonged. Did my mother think that I wanted to climb up and have a slug? Not a chance.

I was put to bed after I had eaten a Stirling's roll. Mmm, I still remember how hot and heavenly it was. My mother had other things on her mind, tired though she was. Yes, my father! Where was he? Clydebank of course – wasn't every fireman in Glasgow there that night? Mind you, anybody who happened to have an unfortunate chimney blaze incurred a hefty fine if it took place during an air raid. While I was asleep, she had been up to Wellshot school only to be told, 'I'm sorry. No word yet Mrs Bernardini.' It was now ten in the morning. 'Just go home,' she was told, 'they should be back soon.'

Would they though?

I was sound asleep when my father came home. Our normal habit when coming up the stairs was to thump the wall on the way up to let my mother know we were there. Dad was so buggered, if you'll excuse the expression, that he wasn't even able to do that. As you might imagine, he was as black as the Earl o' Hell's waistcoat, to quote one of his own expressions. 'Oh, thank goodness you're safe, I've been worried sick,' my mother exclaimed. There were no hugs or kisses; that wasn't the way things were done in those days. Her words were enough to validate their bond. As I went to go through to the room, my mum's warning finger was up. 'Shh. Yer father's sleeping.' One look into the bed recess left me in no doubt.

'Can a huv a piece, ma?'

'Here ye are.' She handed me a roll and jam that she had already prepared, anticipating my request.

'A see ye've got yer shoes on. Are ye goin' oot?'

'Aye.'

'Where are ye goin'?' She always had to ask that.

'Ah'm goin tae look fur shrapnel.'

'Well be sure ye come back when ye hear the bells cos yer daddy will be up an' ready for his tea. Oh an' mind yer hands on these sharp things,' (and believe me they were sharp).

My grandad used to be church officer in the Central church, and it was his job to ring the bells at six o'clock every night, to let the workers at the sandpit know it was time to stop. That night was no exception and as soon as I heard the bells, I made sure I was back for my tea.

'Wash yer hands,' another thing my mother always reminded me to do, 'and don't leave those sharp things on the dresser.'

Over tea I was engrossed in my dad's account of how his section's job was to keep the hoses trained on the *Duke of York*, the heavy battleship that happened to be in dock that night, and a likely target for the Germans. However, for some reason they seemed to be concentrating on the Holy City further up the hill for. We'll never understand why. Of course, in those days bomb-aiming wasn't an exact science.

'Right. Enough talk. Time for bed ma lad. Ah've put your bottle in so it will be warmed up.'

Mothers always knew the right thing to do.

The Home Guard
During the war, my father and uncles on both side of the family were involved to some extent, although in most cases too old to be conscripted for active service. Both uncles on my mother's side served in the forces, one in the Royal Scots in the army of the Rhine in the First World War and the other in the RASC serving in India in 1945. My father was in the AFS, or Auxiliary Fire Service, and played a vital role in the Clydebank blitz. His brother, my uncle Gordon, joined the Home Guard (that of BBC Television's *Dad's Army* fame). They started out as the LDV or Local Defence Volunteers, although a more jocular title

was the 'Look, Duck and Vanishers,' which could easily apply in the story I'm about to relate.

Uncle Gordon was part of an exercise one Saturday, where two opposing sides were separated and told that their mission was to seek out and destroy the other group. The operation covered an area around Parkhead forge, Westmuir Street, Springfield Road and Janefield cemetery and the teams were issued with red and blue armbands respectively. The exercise went on for some considerable time without a result and by late afternoon uncle Gordon decided enough was enough and called on his team to 'repair' to the Straw Hoose, where they could forget the stupid business and get down to some serious drinking. The Straw Hoose was Uncle Gordon's local, from which he had to be 'rescued' on many occasions.

The other team were more conscientious but they too were on the verge of giving up until it suddenly dawned on them. 'Of course! The Straw Hoose. That's where they'll be.' So, after a quick peek through a crack in the door to make sure they were right in their assumption, they charged in, rifles at the ready.

'Right. That's it you lot. Youse are a' deid.'

'Away an' f**k yersels,' said Gordon (he was always good with words my uncle). 'The gem's jegged. We're no playin'.'

So much for defending your country when all you need is a good drink.

School

Back at Wellshot

The evacuation of Dunkirk was a turning point. The phony war was over but the concentrated attacks by the Luftwaffe, the blitz, on London and other English cities was at its height. Britain was to be destroyed in order to make way for the German invasion. The Battle of Britain had begun and wouldn't be over until May 1941; only then would Hermann Goering's boast of annihilating the RAF be dashed. Scotland had been largely ignored but our turn came on that night of 13 March 1941.

I was now back at Wellshot and had stepped up a class or two. All those boys who hadn't been evacuated were back in my class.

'Oh, yer back. Where did ye go tae?' someone inquired.

'I was at ma mammy's auntie up in Carluke.'

'Carluke, where's that?' one of my less-educated classmates asked.

'Oh, it's just up the road.'

Satisfied with that, I resumed friendships and most of my previous teachers were, with a few exceptions, unchanged. My favourite, Miss Ogilvie (of cinnamon-ball treats), remained downstairs with the infants, whom I had outgrown. Lucky them.

I was in and out of Grampa Bernardini's ice-cream shop more frequently now. In his Scots-Italian accent he would say, 'You go fur a paper fur me, a gie you a pocky hat.' I remember my father telling me that Grampa had come to Scotland from Barga with his seven brothers when he was about eight. However, when my cousin Rena and her husband Robert visited us in 1997 she had a very different version of events. According to Rena, Grampa had made the mayor of Barga's daughter pregnant. I think this was a figment of her imagination but, nevertheless, when we visited Barga in 1998 to research our family history, I envisaged a group of the said girl's brothers waiting for us with loaded shotguns. Lucky for us, that didn't happen. Mind you, our enquiries about the Bernardinis didn't come to anything either.

To get back to my old school pals, although some were not so pally now due to unwelcome developments in the war. The chest-beating Italian leader, Benito Mussolini, had decided to become a double act with 'the Great Dictator' himself, Charlie Chaplin. Sorry, let me correct that; I think his name was Adolf something. Anyway, the German–Italian axis gave rise to some hostility towards me among certain boys, none of whom I regarded as friends.

'You're a wee Tally.'

My denial was quick and to the point.

'No, I am not.'

'Your grandfather has got an ice-cream shop an' he comes fae Italy.'

As I was good at geography, and knew that Tuscany was fairly close to Switzerland, I quickly replied, 'No, no. Ma grampa used tae herd sheep for his daddy on the Swiss side of the border.' I'm glad to say they swallowed this explanation and I, being a devout coward, was spared a few thumps. My father said that internment on the Isle of Man might be on the cards. 'Aw no, I'm just back fae Carluke.' The thought did cross my mind, however, that having been to the Isle of Man before, it might be rather enjoyable. I wondered if I would get to sail my yacht on the boating pond or more likely be put behind bars for the duration on a diet of bread and water. Luckily, for one reason or another, we were allowed to stay.

Back home in Tollcross, I had joined the cubs. That was the 102 pack at the corner of Sorby and Westmuir streets. At the end of every meeting we would get down on our hunkers, with two fingers on the ground, and chant:

A-k-e-l-a, we'll do our best,
We'll dib, dib, dib,
We'll dob, dob, dob

Following that little ditty, we would jump up and shout 'woof!', with the first two fingers of our right hand up to our foreheads in the cub salute. Did you ever hear anything as weird as that? It was all thanks to *Jungle Book* by Rudyard Kipling: Akela was the young lady in charge of the pack and her two underlings were Baloo and Bagheera.

The cub pack was divided into groups of six and I ended up a senior sixer, which meant I was in control of one of the sixes, great fun for us young scouts to be. Another thing I recall, was that our cub pack was entered in a competition for percussion and kazoos. You must remember kazoos, wee silver trumpet things with a circular mesh part on top; you put it to your mouth and blew tunes into it. The competition was held in Riddrie parish church hall and although our pack didn't win, I was pleased when I was singled out as best drummer. An indication perhaps of a drumming career to come.

Quali' time

It was coming up to 'Quali' time at school, our nickname for the qualification exam for entry into secondary school. Eastbank was on offer for pupils with medium to low marks, while Whitehill took those who did better in the exam. Don't ask me how but I got into the latter category. Anyway, Whitehill suited me better, but only because I liked the badge and the colours of the uniform. My artistic bent was emerging even then, rather than any form of academic reasoning.

That year Glasgow had a visit from King George V and Queen Mary and I remember all the children being given a white mug with their picture on the front and also a flag, which we had to wave as the royal entourage passed. We sat on the pavement on Tollcross Road waving our flags like mad and bawling out 'hooray, hooray'. It was one of the last memories from my Wellshot days. It would now be onwards and upwards to secondary school.

Whitehill school

Whitehill senior secondary was a totally different experience; subjects separated into categories, with different teachers for each period. All the teachers, while specialists in their subjects, were naturally separated by character and also teaching method. First year wasn't too bad and neither were my results in the end-of-term exam. However, by the time I got into second year I had developed a reputation for my ability to impersonate the teachers. The problem was that my talent for mimicry meant I didn't concentrate enough on my schoolwork. The whole purpose of secondary school was to instil knowledge, allowing pupils either to get a job that matched their abilities, or, if brainy enough, a place at university.

I'm afraid the subjects that appealed to me were those of a less academic nature. Maths I could quickly discount, although geometry, whilst belonging to the same group as arithmetic or algebra, was more manageable due to the graphic elements, which I could just about handle. Latin was a total waste of time, unless I had an aspiration to become a priest. As for science, after the Bunsen burner was lit and we got to work on the Leibig condenser and did all that stuff, it was yawn time. One painful incident I recall – for your amusement, certainly not mine – was when we were going through the life of the butterfly. We had passed the pupa and the larvae stages, and the class was asked to name the final stage. Hands were shooting up all over the room and I was chosen to give the answer.

I shouted out in total innocence, 'Syphilis sir.'

'Out here that boy,' the teacher barked, while the class erupted with raucous laughter. I couldn't think why because I was sure I was right. My hands told me I was wrong.

On a lighter note, I heard that the Glasgow art gallery was offering placements for school pupils to visit and choose something to draw from their large collection of stuffed animals and birds. Whitehill was one of the schools on their list and I was lucky enough to be chosen. Off I went with my sketch pad and pencil, but when I entered the gallery I was overwhelmed by the choice of subjects. I went round and round and round again, dismissing the larger animals, until I finally settled on a swallow. It was probably because it was small enough to fit on my drawing pad but it achieved a 'commended' from the gallery and a credit in the school news sheet.

The debating society

I joined the school debating society. This would surely let me prove to everyone that I could be serious for once, but it wasn't to be. My subject was communism, of all things, and I had applied myself and researched the subject thoroughly. So, there I was on the floor of the debating society holding four pages of well-rehearsed script. All was going to plan and I had got to the page that ended with the words, 'Joseph Stalin was born in Tzaritsyn'. On turning over the page, the next sentence should have begun with a capital A, to read, 'At the age of seventeen, he joined the Bolshevik party.' The mistake I had made was that I didn't have a capital letter in the entire script; so, it now read as, 'Joseph Stalin was born in Tzaritsyn at the age of seventeen'. This evoked derisory oohs and chortles of laughter from certain quarters.

My career in the debating society was over before it got started.

Everything went downhill after that and I even had to repeat my second year. I was a failure. No wonder with the marks I got. Maths, as expected, were atrocious: 50/80 for geometry, which was fair, but 8/100 for arithmetic – I think I got one question right on that paper – and, to crown it all, 3/100 for algebra. It might as well have been Greek. And I only managed a 3 because I put my name at the top of the paper! The rest of my marks – for geography, history, English and Latin – proved that I had a brain in there somewhere. Art couldn't save me, despite getting 95/100. When my mother was asked to come and see the head-master, Mr Weir, to ascertain how I might be dishonourably discharged before I infected the rest of the pupils.

So off I went into the wide world, free at last to make my way in a career that would involve the thing I did best: drawing.

My stage career

My mother thought it would be a good idea if I went to tap-dancing lessons. Mabel Neil's dancing school was a good place to learn and she ran classes in the Fullarton hall on Saturday mornings. I took to it like a duck – not to water but to treacle, at first at any rate. But as soon as my left foot knew what my right was doing, I got into the swing and after a while began to enjoy it. Mabel ran three classes: tap, Highland and ballet. Her boyfriend was Polish, by the name of Jan Rogowski, and he took charge of the ballet classes, being an ex-ballet dancer himself. Not for me though, that cissy stuff, although, as it happened, my short legs couldn't reach the practice bar, so that clinched it.

Mr Mooney ran the Highland and tap classes and he came every week, all the way from Cloberhill Road in Knightswood and brought his daughter Irene along with him. He must have recognised potential in my tap-dancing because he persuaded Mabel to pair Irene and me in a tap routine that he had devised for the next concert, which was to be held in the Lyric theatre. We had to share a dressing room with loads of young dancers in the chorus line so it was quite congested. Irene's mother made sure to protect her daughter from anyone's gaze as we changed into our stage costumes; there were obvious changes taking place in Irene's figure, even if they were minimal. So, with make-up duly applied, we were ready. Nervous, but ready. I had white long trousers, a brown shirt and white bow tie; she wore a dazzling pink dress with sequins that would sparkle in the foot-lights and red tap shoes with large pink bows. When our turn came, and the chorus line parted, we launched into our routine.

Me:

I like New York in June,
How about you?

Tapi, tipi, tapi-ti-tap.
Her:

I like a Gershwin tune,
How about you?

Tapi, tipi tapi-ti-tap,
Her:

I love a fireside, when a storm is doo

Notice the American accent here; authenticity was everything!
Me:

I like potato chips

Her:

Moonlight and motor trips

. . . as we slid together cheek to cheek

How about you?

This was showbusiness. Dancing and singing as well! Fred Astaire and Ginger Rodgers. How are ya? Our performance was received with rapturous applause, well at least from our mothers standing in the wings. Broadway here we come. Unfortunately for us, perhaps fortunately for them, there were no ships going in the direction of the legendary Great White Way. All available ships were deployed in convoys, bringing much-need food to wartime Britain.

We only performed that routine once more. It was at a venue in Knightswood, where Mr Mooney was proud to show off his daughter's prowess, and mine, to a home audience. Irene looked stunning in her outdoor clothes that day; she wore a lovely coat with fur round the bottom and a white, Cossack-style hat with two baubles in front, one red, the other white. That's me again with my fascination with style. Maybe I should have been a fashion designer.

The Scouts

It was 1943 and I had joined the Scouts. There wasn't a troop near us but there was a lad who worked in the GEC beside my dad called Andy Henry. He lived in Academy Street and he said

I could join his troop, the 35th, which met up at Cemetery Road on Friday nights. It was quite far away but no problem for me; down the stairs two at a time and away up through Sandyhills and onto Springboig. They played some rough-and-tumble games in the Scouts, which didn't really suit me as I was small and could come in for some bashings. Other pursuits demanded brainpower, like observation, in which a tray full of assorted objects would be brought out, the purpose being to remember them, and, when the tray was removed, to name them. I liked that game. There were knots, of course, and first aid and other games as well.

The part I liked best was the campfire at the end of the night. Not a real fire of course, being inside the hall, but we would sit round in a circle and sing songs, some of which had a distinct flavour of the Transvaal thanks to Baden Powell's days in the army there; it was where he got the idea of starting the Scout movement. Songs with words like, 'Ging, gang, goolee, goolee, vatchla, ging, gang, goo, ging, gang, goo,' and other popular ditties from the African veldt. Then there were rounds like 'London's burning', which I liked because it was more harmonious. Another favourite was, 'We're riding along on the crest of a wave and the sun is in the sky', made popular by Ralph Reader of Boy Scout gang shows fame.

Scout troops were divided into patrols and I was assigned to the peewits. I would much rather have been in the lions or tigers, but at least I liked the patrol leader, whose name was Glen Peters. He lived in Sandyhills and I was able to accompany him, especially on dark nights, before running home to Tollcross. Bill Gordon was the scoutmaster and Bob Morrow the assistant scoutmaster. I mention Bob because he was a talented artist and had been given the job of decorating the walls of one of the upstairs rooms in Scout headquarters at 21 Elmbank Street. What's more, it was unique in that he had used fluorescent paint, which would appear as an eerie, luminous glow when the room was dark. Bob lived in Mount Vernon, and, knowing I liked to draw, he invited me to his house, where he introduced me to a form of modelling. He would show me how to make faces out of a type of plaster called pyruma. I was hopeless at this and after saying goodbye to his mother, I would leave his house clutching a bag of unrecognisable plaster faces that invariably came to a pitiful end in our dustbin. Poor Bob, he did his best to make a Henry Moore out of me but without success I'm sorry to say. Soon after, he emigrated to New Zealand to pursue a career as an animator with Miramar films and that was the last I saw of him.

I had always worn the kilt and sporran, ever since I was a small boy; the waistband would start life coming up to my chest and end up above my knees as I grew into them. So, all that I needed was the rest of my uniform from Scout headquarters: neckerchief, shirt, lanyard, whistle, hat and the very necessary red stockings. These were the distinguishing feature that made the 35th stand out from the other troops in the Glasgow area.

Wearing a kilt through to my early teens became normal and I didn't give it a second thought. I used to keep bumping into this man in Shettleston when I least expected it. He was the scoutmaster of a Sea Scout troop and he would tell me about weekend camps they had down at Saltcoats and asked if I would like to come along. He came across as a nice man, but it did seem odd that he managed to turn up in front of me so often. When I told my mother, she said, 'oh that was very nice of him,' but he was known to our own scoutmaster and my mother was quickly informed that he wasn't to be trusted. I was told to avoid him, an instruction I obeyed without question and the matter was dropped.

That was the first of three encounters. The next was more frightening.

I was coming home from school one day and running upstairs when I became conscious of a man behind me. He asked if I knew so and so up this close and I was about to answer him when his hand went up my kilt and he muttered something about tonight. It was a windy day, and, fortunately, the lavatory door on the first landing, just above us, rattled loudly. Thinking there was somebody about to come out, he panicked and took to his heels, shouting as he went, 'Nine o'clock the night, roon the back. Right.'

I was no sooner in the house before my mother found me a chore.

'Don't take off your jacket. I want you to go for potatoes.'

'Oh mum. Ah'm just in.'

'Now!'

'But ah've got homework to do.'

She had never seen me so keen to start homework.

'What's wrong with you today?

'Nothing.'

I couldn't think of any more excuses. There was nothing else for it, so I crept down the stairs expecting the worst at every landing. Luckily, the coast was clear. The words paedophiles and stalkers hadn't entered the English language in those days, so this was out of the ordinary and neither my mother nor I had ever been confronted with this type of situation before.

On the same subject, my mother used to see this fine-looking gentleman dressed in the kilt as he strode down Tollcross Road. He was always in full Highland dress with the crossed lacing up the stockings, *Sgian Dhubh*, lovely belt and sporran; the lot. He wore a different tartan every time and she was in awe of him. One day we met him on the street and he complimented me on how well I looked in my kilt. We got talking, and he said he had any number of kilts, some of which he'd outgrown. If I would like to call at his house, he would let me have one. My mother thought it a very generous offer, never for a moment thinking that this nice man could be in the same mould as the creep who interfered with me on the stair.

Around this time, I was taking drumming lessons from a man called Alec McCormick, who was the leading drummer with the City of Glasgow Police pipe band and he happened to live two stairs up in Rockdove Mansions, just above this 'lovely man.' One day after practice, I was in the kitchen talking to Alec's wife, Peggy, and I was telling her about the man downstairs and his kind offer of a kilt. Alec came through at that point, having put away the ironing board that we used for practice, just as Peggy was trying to suppress her surprise at my disclosure. As soon as she told him, both of them burst out laughing, with Alec wagging his finger, telling me, 'No, no!'

After that I always walked quickly past his door on the way up the stairs to my drumming lessons. When I got home and told my (still innocent) mother, she couldn't believe it. 'He was such

Jean and Peter's wedding day

Me and three roon the back of 1060

Age 6 at Largs

Morning wash at Leeside Cottage

Age 10 at Stanley station

Mum and I at
Leeside Cottage

The Merry Eight

The Deerpark Choir

As KoKo in *The Mikado*

Bing, Ann and Tina home from IOM

Tina on her way to work

Flight 15 at Bridgnorth

Miserable Xmas at North Pickenham

Present for my 21st birthday

Showing off the sparkler

Marriage send-off

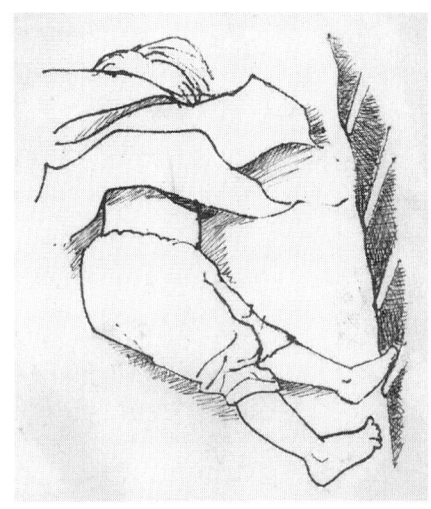

Linsey asleep

The happy couple

Dear ol' Austin

Linsey AKA Sheena Wilson

At work on my stairhead studio

Painting of Bowmore 1962

World Champions Edinburgh 1953

At my desk at Rex Publicity

a nice man too.' It was a lesson learnt. Having been oblivious about men like that we had been brought face to face with reality.

My first summer camp with the scouts was in Aviemore. Today Aviemore is a bustling ski resort but in 1942 it was a quiet village, nothing more than a train halt between Grantown on Spey and Inverness. Our campsite was situated near the shores of Loch Morlich, about two miles from the village. The field where we settled would normally have been a peaceful spot but this was wartime and the 51st Highland Division, including a cavalry detachment, was in training just along the tree-lined road from us. Every morning, we were treated to the clip-clop of horse's hooves, together with their neighs and snorts as they trooped down the road for a day's training.

I wasn't used to camp life, with so many outdoor tasks to be undertaken. It was a particularly hot summer, which meant that our tents had to be 'brailed' each morning. Cottage tents as they were called, which would become our homes for the fortnight, had two-foot-deep walls of canvas all around, which had to be rolled and tied up to meet the sloping tent roofs in order to let the air blow through, a process known as brailing. Another task was digging deep holes in the forest for use as latrines; I was handed a spade, with the bigger lads assigned as supervisors. Washing our underwear every second day was obligatory; we used the rocks in the river to bash our clothes in a manner similar to women in hot countries. Boys being boys, we did our fair share of splashing each other at the same time.

We enjoyed other scouting pursuits. There were visits to Aviemore, where we could buy tea and scones at the Pot Luck tearoom, trips to Loch Morlich for swims, and, of course, the nightly campfire with songs and stories, which I liked but also brought on a wee bout of homesickness.

One thing sticks in my head, quite literally, about that first camp. We had to bring our own rations and just before getting on to the train at the start of our journey, my bag of sugar developed a hole in the bottom. Now sugar, being one of the most valuable wartime commodities, had to be saved by any means possible. The best receptacle was my scout hat, which was fine to begin with, if a tad unhygienic. This didn't deter us scouts, oh no. Our motto after all was 'be prepared'. However, by the end of the first week, the inside of my new scout hat had become really sticky, due to the daily dipping-in of wet spoons by almost everyone on camp. The stickiness became even more unbearable when I was obliged to wear it to church parade on the middle Sunday. I came home more grown up after those two weeks. Very brown, but with an even darker-brown halo of sticky sugar round my head. Don't mention Aviemore to me again.

There were other summer camps while I was in the 35th, each with its own memory. Largo was next, but it was a washout as it rained nearly every day. We camped in Upper Largo, which meant a trek down to Lower Largo and the sea. The attraction was the statue erected to the memory of Andrew Selkirk, the sailor marooned on a desert island in the South Pacific for over four years, and the inspiration for the novel, *Robinson Crusoe*, by Daniel Defoe. The statue of this bearded gent was of little interest to us scouts except for the pistol stuck in his belt. In our boyish imaginings we speculated about whether he actually used it to kill the natives, thus rendering the island uninhabited.

Unlike Aviemore, there was very little brailing to be done except on the odd day when the rain stopped for a while. The senior scouts, doing their duty as cooks, had their work cut out keeping the large cooking pots, or Dixies as they were called, from filling up with rainwater at mealtimes. Once more our motto, 'be prepared', came in handy as the cooks managed to find a way round the deluges. We were always so hungry that it didn't matter how the food tasted; down it went regardless.

Next year it was Coldingham, a pretty little town on the east coast, just north of Eyemouth. There isn't much that I remember about that summer camp except that the weather was pretty good. We didn't suffer the torrential rain we had at Largo but neither were we blessed with the hot days of Aviemore. One thing that I remember about Coldingham was that during a game of football, Bill Gordon, our scoutmaster, had to be carried off the field having suffered a broken arm, which meant it was in a sling for the rest of the week. That was a blow, not only to his arm, but also to the troop. He was the best cook in the camp.

Auchengillan, near the West Highland Way, was a great weekend camping spot for scouts from all over the city, so much so that in the 1940s it felt like a mini jamboree. It is now a fully established outdoor centre and hosted the official scout jamboree in 2017. We went there for training, hoping to qualify for another badge for our arm while also taking part in some great scouting activities.

One not so memorable break was when a friend and I went for a weekend's camping in a field up the glen from Fairlie, south of Largs. My father had reminded me to say hello to my gran's sister, who lived there, something I wasn't keen on because

I didn't know her. The rain came down in sheets when we got there and needless to say we were having a miserable time. We couldn't even light a fire to cook on and had to rely on the sandwiches and biscuits we had brought with us, along with tins of cold baked beans. It was a disaster until I had the bright idea of calling on my great aunt; anything would be better than another plateful of cold beans. We presented ourselves at her door and I used my good name to cement relations right away.

'Come away in you two. Where huv ye been? Campin' up there in this weather? My goodness, yer like a pair o' droon't rats.'

My mother couldn't have put it better. In we went.

'Get these wet claes aff, the two o' ye.'

I didn't expect this. Clothes dried in front of a roaring fire. Now back in our scout uniforms, we were treated to something new: stovies, manna from heaven and no one could cook them like my dad's aunt.

The Mikado

This event was to have a profound influence on my life. I was eleven years of age when our Scout troop, the 35th, joined forces with the 21st Girl Guides from Eastbank church to stage *The Mikado*. It was an ambitious project for a group of untrained singers and actors, from my age up to seventeen. Our scouts were assembled in Sandyhills bowling club one evening where we had to sing various songs, supposedly for fun. Little did we realise that we were being assessed by qualified singers, who walked around as we sang and singled out those they considered suitable for principal roles in the opera.

A week later we met again and the choice was narrowed down. This time, the chosen few were asked to stay behind and sing again, solo this time. I had a very high voice as did another boy of a similar age, then a few of the older boys, whose voices had already broken, were separated again. The whittling down continued until we were finally dismissed with a 'don't call us, we'll call you' approach. When I got home I was quizzed by my parents about what part I had got, but there was nothing to tell. All I could do was wait.

Two more weeks went by. Then another meeting was called, again in Sandyhills bowling club, but this time we were joined by the Guides, thirty-six of them, twenty-five of us. This was the full cast for a huge undertaking, one that would become a big part of our lives for the next year. But first there was the small matter of deciding which roles we would play. Because librettos had been handed out at the start of the evening, we knew only too well that there are only nine principal characters in *The Mikado*. It was time to find out if I would be playing one.

The room fell silent as the names were announced.

The part of the Mikado was announced first and this was given to Bob Morrow, the assistant scoutmaster (remember he was the talented artist who did those luminous murals in Scout headquarters). Next came the part of Nanki Poo of 'A wandering minstrel' fame, and son of the Mikado. This part was divided between two boys, who would take alternate nights over a run of six nights. Then came the part of Ko Ko, a cheap tailor who later got promoted to Lord High Executioner over Pooh Bah, who became Lord High everything else.

When my name was announced, for the part of KoKo, the first thing that came into my head was, 'I wonder if I would get to learn Japanese'. At least it would be better than the boring Latin I was having to take at Whitehill. All the other principal parts were read out and applauded. Then came the schoolgirls, nobles, guards and coolies, who made up the chorus. Thank goodness I wouldn't have to stand in the crowd at the back flicking a wee fan up and down. I would have an axe to carry.

Miyasama ter miyasama omnimanomayenee

You see, I was right, we were learning Japanese. This was the song that heralded the entrance of the Mikado. It was an important song, the main theme in the overture. It involved the whole cast, while the man himself strode on to the stage, or I should say, the school floor, because we had changed our rehearsal venue to Shettleston school to give us more room to move around. We were all given cheap little fans in order to familiarise ourselves with them. (I wonder how many of you ladies have ever used one, other than at a fancy-dress party. The trick is to hold it up while closed, and then flick it down very fast to open it, at the same time turning the side with the Japanese picture out towards the audience and then fluttering it like mad.)

Rehearsals were going along nicely. It was now spring and the chorus songs were being thrashed out and sounding quite satisfactory, according to our musical director, Mr Hadden. He was also working with the principals on their solos, including myself. We were all beginning to hear them in our heads as we went about our daily lives, which was good. Not so good though when they kept popping in and out of my head during those Latin classes – *amo, amas, amat, amamus, amatis* . . . 'awandringminstrel I, a thing of shreds and patches'.

Oops, *amant*. I wouldn't mind, but that wasn't even my song!

One of the distractions in rehearsals was Helen Thomson. She was in the chorus and I fancied her, but it was one of those brief-eye-contact-and-faint-smile relationships. Helen lived in Sandyhills and I would make a point, each time I passed her house, of walking very slowly, hoping to see her at the window. Then I would start loudly to whistle one of Koko's well-known songs from the opera, to let her know it was me.

On a tree by a river a little tom tit sang willow tit willow tit willow.

Her mother would probably be sitting there saying. 'There's that silly wee bugger fae the scouts daien his Romeo again.' Little did she know she was dealing with the Lord High Executioner and I could have felled her with 'one swift blow of my axe'. Sadly, however, my Juliet never responded to her Romeo. Rehearsals continued well into autumn without a break and by now I was really enjoying it.

Our performance was scheduled to take place in the Lyric theatre, (long since gone) off Renfield Street, from 23–28 October All the other principals had understudies except the Mikado, played by Bob, and KoKo by me. This meant that we had to perform every night instead of every other night. I didn't mind because once I knew my lines, six nights or three, it didn't really matter. I remember counting the number of words I would have to say, not including songs, and it came to 1,264. Not a problem when you are eleven I suppose. The problem would arise closer to the performance.

It was now mid-October and I was developing a cold. My mother, conscious of the fact that it was coming up to 'show-time', nevertheless ordered me to bed.

'But what about *The Mikado* mum?'

'Never mind that. It's bed for you my lad.'

Alarm bells were ringing now so much so that Bill Gordon, our scoutmaster, came to the house and pleaded with my mother to allow me to sing. I had no understudy and the show had to go on. Thanks to the power of Vick stuffed up my nose, and over my chest and back, I was able to make it in time for the dress rehearsal.

In the meantime, our costumes had arrived courtesy of D'Oyly Carte. The only thing was how do we wear them? We soon found out and we all loved getting into the Japanese gear and squeezing into those bald wigs. I was disappointed to discover that there was no big axe in the package that arrived from their costume department. There were only a few lovely big fans for use by the principals, and mine sure was big. But because of all that training we did with the cheap stuff, this would be easy. The orchestra, yes, a whole orchestra, was tuning up in the pit and the empty theatre buzzing with excitement. When we were into our costumes and make up, we were lucky enough to have a picture taken for the press.

I still had to get through the week without coughing and spluttering. By the second and third nights, my medication seemed to be working, together with a pocket full of Zubes, remember them?

During the length of the performance, we sang for some pretty important people, like the chief commissioner for Scouts in Glasgow and his opposite number from the Girl Guides Association. There were delegations from other Scout troops and Girl Guide companies from all over Glasgow. Unfortunately, the King and Queen couldn't make it due to some other engagement. At least that's what they said, but you know them! Otherwise I might have been knighted for services to executions.

One person who *was* there, was the theatre critic for the *Glasgow Herald,* Arthur Meikle. He was my English teacher and also happened to be a customer in my aunt May's newsagents in Cathcart. Now you might have thought that I would have been acknowledged by him in some way during class or in the school corridor. A raised eyebrow perhaps, a wink or even a knowing nod would have done, but no. Was my performance *that bad*? Was he perhaps there the night my throat could have deteriorated in quality due to my condition? I never found out. I never even saw his critique in the paper. Just as well I suppose.

Overall our performance of *The Mikado* turned out to be a most enjoyable and memorable year for me and I'm sure for all the others who took part in it.

The sad thing is, my voice would never be the same again.

When it was over *The Mikado* left a void, not only for me but also for the rest of the cast. After a while, I was persuaded to go for an audition at the BBC for a programme they were planning. My father knew this older man, a singer/pianist, whom he asked to give me the benefit of his experience. He thought it would be nice for me to sing something Scottish, so after rummaging through a pile of songs from his piano stool, he pulled out 'Bonny Mary of Argyll'. This was obviously a favourite of his, but not of mine. A more unsuitable song for someone of my age you couldn't imagine. He should have chosen one of the songs from *The Mikado*, which, by this time, were embedded in my brain. However, I felt obliged to go along with this unlikely tutor's advice.

I presented myself at Queen Margaret Drive and in the studio was faced with a microphone, which I had never used before, plus a panel of judges, another new experience. When I had finished, there was polite applause. The producer, Mr Howard Lockhart, came over and asked me a few questions about how long I had been singing. I told him about my part in *The Mikado* and the cold I had suffered and so on. He said he was sorry to tell me that I had failed the audition, not due to poor singing but because of something no one had mentioned before. My voice was breaking and I shouldn't be speaking for long, much less singing, for the next three months. It was a blow. There I was, silenced for the foreseeable future.

Now that all the excitement of the past year had died down, it was back to my drawing and model-making. I would go in and gawk for ages at the beautiful aeroplanes that had been made from kits in the window of the Clyde Model Dockyard in the Argyll arcade. One day, a real aeroplane came to town in the form of a Short Stirling bomber, which was displayed in George Square. Lady Rachel McRoberts, a wealthy woman who had lost three sons serving in the RAF, donated £25,000 to buy a bomber to honour their deaths, and here it was, aptly named 'McRoberts Reply', with the name clearly written on the side. I joined the long queue of people and at last was able to climb up to touch it, look in the cockpit and imagine all the heroic goings-on. Forget *The Mikado*, this was the chance I'd been waiting for all my life. I was there, I was flying it and I went home fulfilled.

It was a lovely day so I was able to get home, get into the sannies, grab my tennis racquet with my two well-worn tennis balls covered in red dust, inside a net slung over it. I was off to the park to pursue my latest interest in life: 4*d* for forty minutes worth of fun before the whistle went and we had to leave the court. The two men who watched from the box were called Bobby and Eddie. Bobby, always referred to as 'wee Bobby', was great and listened to our patter with a smile on his face. Eddie, on the other hand, was more serious and kept us under control if we got unruly, which we often did. We would stand there, anxiously champing at the bit, waiting for the courts to be rolled and lined with white chalk. We just couldn't wait to hand over our money and get out there.

Wimbledon it wasn't, but wonderful it was.

The Winchin' Years

Winchin'

Winchin' is a common Glasgow term for courting. Way back in the Forties it was an uncomplicated affair, with nothing too serious going on. I never even went out with a girl on my own; it was always in a crowd. Usually on a Sunday night on long walks – and I mean long. We would cover miles without noticing the distance, as we would be too busy laughing and joking, enjoying each other's company. At the same time, we made sure that we weren't too far away from someone we fancied. There was always somebody recounting a funny incident from the previous week, usually to do with tennis, as most of us were members of Deerpark tennis club. It was all innocent fun. The word 'sex' never entered the conversation.

A few of us became members of the choir, a great group of singers who met on Friday nights in Wellshot Road school. But that wasn't enough; every chance we got, we'd gather and sing into the dusk at the park gates after the tennis had finished, on a summer's evening. As far as I recall, hardly anyone read staff notation. The music we were given was always printed in Sol-fah (that's doh-ray-me-fah-soh-type music by the way). Bobby

Gardner was our conductor and he had a great way of getting the best out of us. We were modelled on the Glasgow Orpheus Choir and sang a lot of arrangements by Hugh Roberton, such as 'All in the April Evening', 'The Isle of Mull' and the 'Dashing White Sergeant'.

I looked forward to Friday nights, not just because of the singing, which I loved, but also because of another love growing in my heart. She was a soprano and the soprano section sat right in front of the tenors, of which I was a member. Her name was Tina Brown and she was also a good tennis player, which I admired, because I was mediocre and would never reach the dizzy heights of the first team. Tina, however, went on not only to win the ladies singles on a few occasions but also to play for Glasgow public parks in the doubles with her partner, Elma Condie.

But back to the choir. Our concert, held in the Wellshot hall each spring, was the culmination of the hard work we put in during the previous year and would also include sketches and solos and the like. Not being content to take part in these extras, I formed a little singing group of my own, consisting of anyone who could sing from the Sunday-night walking crowd. We were called the Merry Eight, which naturally included Tina. I would write the harmonies, in sol-fa of course, the only way I knew how, and we practised on a Sunday afternoon in Ruth Diamond's house in Shettleston Road. Ruth played the piano and was a great extemporiser rather than a strict play-by-the-music-type pianist. This suited me because she could play anything I threw at her, adding the right chords and making it sound great. My kind of pianist.

Serious winchin'

Tina and I soon became recognised as an item, to use today's parlance. We started winchin' every Wednesday night. She lived on the ground floor of the close and I would stand outside and listen for her door shutting. Once she came out, we would be off, arm in arm, up the road to our weekly venue, the State cinema in Shettleston. I would push the boat out by producing a packet of Spangles for her, and then we would stand in the picture queue, in all weathers, before entering into that magical world of plush carpeting, soft lighting and polished chrome bars. Once inside, we wouldn't be happy until we could get up to the back row. That's where the 'chummies' were – seats made to accommodate two people, and much sought after by us winchin' couples. I don't need to explain why! Once we had found our chummie, we were there for the night.

'Surely that's no John Wayne leadin' the 7th Cavalry into Monument Valley – again!' All too soon, the picture would end and we would disengage from our heavenly clinch. We were almost always too late to make it out in time so we had to stand, bleary eyed, until the national anthem, or 'The King' as it was referred to in those days, was over. Another shilling's-worth of darkness well spent; actually, 1s 9d each, plus the spangles. That was my pocket money gone for the week. But what the hell, I was in love. Home we went, arms linked and happy as Larry, hoping to get into the back close before Tina's sister and her boyfriend got there. Mind you, sometimes we got lucky as they varied their nights.

We had to get that last winch in before we parted.

In the Fifties, the Isle of Man was my destination of choice for holidays. The first year we went to Port Erin, and the following year to Douglas. Two couples, Ann Shearer, Bill Crosbie (aka Bing), Tina and me. The holiday to Port Erin was in 1953, the year I was forced to join the other three a day later, as my pipe band, the Clan Macrae Society, in which I was a drummer, was competing in the world championships in Edinburgh on the Saturday. While I was sorry I couldn't travel with them, it was well worth it; we won the trophy, and one happy drummer stepped off the plane on the Sunday to join the other three. We had a wonderful holiday that year, mostly engaged in friendly battles on the tennis courts, and, after suitable replenishment, it was back to the boarding house for the night.

It must sound innocent to the modern reader, but after our goodnight kisses we retired to our separate double rooms for the night, a bit of a contrast to what went on during the lads' holiday in fifty-two. I am glad to say, however, that during those two weeks, I resisted all temptation and stayed faithful to my true love. Port Erin was good, clean, memorable, sporty fun.

RAF years

I had gone through many happy years from the age of 15; happy in my job, happy with my social life and happy that I had found the love of my life. As I approached my eighteenth birthday all that was about to change. George V1 would be requesting my presence in the form of compulsory National Service, which at the time was for eighteen months. It was an interruption I wasn't too happy about. I had worked alongside my immediate boss, Ken McLaren, for the previous three years, and he had been a great influence on me. He was an ardent follower of the likes of Douglas Young, C. M. Grieve and Wendy Wood, founder of the

Scottish National Party. I got it into my head that I should be a conscientious objector on the grounds that I didn't want to fight for England; I was Scottish by birth and proud of it. My parents weren't pleased by my decision, fearing a possible prison sentence. In the end, for their sakes, I relented, and in due course, offered my services to the RAF. Of the three services it was my first choice, given I had always liked aeroplanes. I was to report to Padgate, near Warrington, where our first breakfast consisted of one hard-boiled egg. Surely that wasn't what the rest of the station was given for breakfast?

After a week in Padgate, I was posted to Bridgnorth in Shropshire for my initial eight weeks of training, or square bashing as it was more accurately called. We were divided into huts, which held about forty of us, with a corporal in charge. Corporal Moore – an Irishman from Eire, would you believe – was our drill instructor, or 'DI' as they were known. Their function was to terrorise us into submission upon their command. All the lads were now officially termed airmen and addressed as such by the DIs. The DIs wore skipped caps pulled down at the front, which gave them an even more menacing appearance when they addressed you, man to man. I was always 'airman Barandini'. Moore never called me by my proper name even when I was brave, or foolish, enough to correct him.

'It's Bernardini, corporal.'

'Right Barandini.'

I was a marked man from that moment. He might have been putting it on because he liked the sound of 'Barandini', or perhaps he was stubborn and wanted to prove that he knew best. I didn't argue.

The station had a brass band and I was lucky enough to become the drummer. This was a disadvantage in many respects as it marked me out from the rest of the lads in the eyes of Corporal Moore. Now, I would not only have to blanco my webbing, but also polish my brass drum and blanco the ropes on it as well, while taking my turn at polishing the coal in the large tub and 'blancoing' round the top of the large rectangular skip that stood in the middle of the hut. Sometimes, the corporal would have me polish his shoes in his private room, which was at the end of the billet. For this duty the DIs were obliged to give you payment in return; often, this might be something as trivial as a sweet, but it still came under the reward category. Another rule was that as we marched to the dining hall we had to chant, 'Mars are marvellous, Mars are marvellous' in time to our marching step. It was to give us an appetite, as if we needed any help with that.

My eight weeks of square-bashing was over, with a forty-eight-hour pass halfway through, and I got the chance to see Tina again. We all waited eagerly to find out where our permanent posting would take us. I was hoping mine would be in Scotland. Rumours abounded of 15 Flight (that was us) being posted to Korea. It was just a rumour, for which I gave thanks. The postings were read out, 'Johnson – West Kirby, Ponsonby – Hereford, McElwinny – East Fortune'. Lucky devil, that wasn't far from Falkirk. Then it was my turn, 'Bernardini – 281 MU North Pickenham.'

'Oh no, not Norfolk!'

As the title suggests, 281 MU was a maintenance unit with not an aeroplane in sight. It was at the arse end of nowhere and even Norwich, the biggest town, was twenty-five miles away. So much for a flying station. North Pickenham had been operational during the war but now all it had was a disused control tower and empty runways with bombs stacked up all the way along. The equipment section, to which I was assigned, was divided into two, one for clothing and one for technical stuff, from nuts and bolts to engine parts. This was known as the R & D (receipts and dispatches) and I was in charge of it, with a Nissan hut all to myself. I was a storeman now. Great. The job I'd always wanted!

One day Flying Officer Barnes came in on his rounds as duty officer. He was a tall man with glasses and a look-down-his-nose air.

'Sir,' I stood to attention.

'Stand easy. Well how is R&D today Bernardini?'

At least he knew how to pronounce my name.

I was bored and lonely as there wasn't much to do that day and I thought I would offer a quip.

'Not bad, sir. It's got a slight cold but it should be all right by tomorrow.'

I stupidly thought it might get a chuckle in response, but nothing.

'Carry on Bernardini,' and off he went on his rounds, hands behind his back, leaving me to cast my eyes round the store to make sure nothing was missing.

When work was over for the day, we had to trek a mile to our living quarters, a large Nissan hut. In the evenings there wasn't much to do except read, play cards or something similar. Cards were not for me so I would either write a letter to

Tina, or else draw, at the other end of the table. Having a reputation for impersonating the officers on the station, I would often be goaded into performing on top of the table, much to the amusement of my roommates. At the weekends those who were lucky enough to live within a short train distance would be off home to places like Yarmouth or London. But I never wanted to go to the capital, because that was where the man who got me here in the first place lived and he wasn't exactly a friend so to speak.

Sports day came around every Wednesday afternoon and we got the chance to play our chosen sport. Mine was tennis, and we would climb into the back of a 3-ton truck called a Garry and be driven to Swaffham where courts had been reserved. It was a break from routine and quite enjoyable. The sergeant in charge was a decent chap and a good tennis player himself or at least he had been in his youth.

It was at Swaffham that I was able to watch the B29s as they flew overhead while coming in to land at USAF Lakenheath. The United States Airforce were soon to move into a station close to us and they would take turns at guard duty up at the work site, as we did. The only difference was that while we would carry 303 rifles over our shoulders with no ammunition in them, the Yanks had loaded carbines and passed the time by taking pot-shots at rabbits. They zipped up and down past our guardroom in their jeeps, to fill up with petrol from one of our bowsers. The jeep had a metal strip, which separated the wind-screen from the bonnet, and as this was the same height from the ground as the entrance barrier, they didn't need to wait for the guard to open it. They would simply drive slowly up to the bar then step on the gas to swing it open themselves and whizz through with a nonchalant wave to the guard.

I decided to hitchhike from Norfolk to Glasgow, on a forty-eight-hour pass, to see my beloved. It took me twenty-four of the forty-eight to get there travelling on twelve different modes of transport, including a Bentley, finishing my journey on the back of a bouncing open lorry that picked me up somewhere in the Borders and dropped me off at my close. I had written to tell Tina to stand in the shop doorway across the road on Saturday evening at seven o'clock. After that final hitch on the back of the open truck, I was dead beat and had gone to bed at three in the afternoon, not even telling my mother about my date as I really thought I would be awake by the time I had told her. I couldn't believe it when my mother looked in on me. It was ten at night and poor Tina had been waiting all that time, even refusing offers from my passing friends to take her to the Darby café to wait in comfort in case I showed up.

If only she had come up the stairs and knocked at the door. But she hadn't met my mother at that stage in our romance and it was understandable as she didn't know what kind of reception she would get. My mother would have been surprised but I'm sure it would have been a pleasant one. After all they had to meet at some stage and that was as good a time as any. We did get a short time to look into each other's eyes in the Darby café after all, such is the power of true love, and we managed to be together for five sublime hours out of the forty-eight. We said goodbye on a platform at Central station at two on the Sunday, with Tina only letting go of my hand when she couldn't run fast enough to keep up with the train. Was it worth it? Of course. It took me a long time to forgive my mother for letting me sleep so long but I should have remembered to tell her.

Every airman on the station was obliged to take a turn as duty storeman. This included being called upon to act as petrol attendants at any time, day or night, over a twenty-four-hour period. Whilst on my watch, I was aroused from a sound sleep one night by the light of the torch carried by the station policeman, or SPs as they were called. I quickly donned warm clothes and made my way to the work site where one of these US airmen needed petrol (at two in the morning of all times). I thought I had swung open the doors at the back of the petrol bowser, but in the pitch dark I chose the wrong bowser, with the result that he got a tank full of diesel instead. This didn't go down well with either my superiors or the USAF and to avoid an international incident, I was put on a charge and quick-marched in to face the presiding officer.

'Left right, left right, left right, left right. Halt.'

'2474269 AC Bernardini.'

'Sir.'

'You are hereby charged with dereliction of duty . . . blah, blah, blah . . . seven days confined to barracks. March him out, sergeant.'

Left right, left right, left right, left right, and I was out with no chance to defend my actions. Not that it would have done any good. Why hadn't I chosen the Navy? Mind you, seven days scrubbing a deck wouldn't have been much fun either.

I thought I would be back to a civilian existence by the end of November 1951, having served my designated eighteenth months, but the powers that be had decided to increase the duration of National Service to two years, which meant I wouldn't be free of this lot until 31 May 1952. To add insult to injury they decided out of the goodness of their hearts to give the regular airmen a pay rise. How unfair was that? I would have to make do with a break for New Year then back to unhappy valley for the next six months. Christmas was just around the corner and while the English airmen took their Christmas break, us heathens had to stay and look after the station in their absence.

I had a good pal who worked in the central registry office at the station. He was Scottish, from Alexandria in Dunbartonshire, by the name of Willie Donal. Willie knew a few Scottish songs so we passed many pleasant hours over that Christmas break practising them, with me singing harmony. I lost touch with Willie, the last I heard he had moved to Bellshill. When I passed through there on a bus tour, I made enquiries about him, but without success; such a shame as we were great buddies. Soon we were off on our New Year break and that was magic. I got to spend time with Tina again and we had a great first footing and all that goes with it. We did the rounds of our tennis-club friends, including Jean Leighton, who lived at the top of Altyre Street. Their house was full of revellers and as we were running out of stuff, we took what we had brought in as a first foot away with us, to go on to the next house. It was all part of the fun and Jean didn't mind. That is, if she ever knew.

With only five months of my National Service remaining, I could at least begin to look forward to the end of my compulsory incarceration in that isolated part of the country. My demobilisation date of the thirtieth of May soon became a reality, enabling me to return to my chosen career at last.

Turning 21

My twenty-first birthday was held in our kitchen at 1060 Tollcross Road on 31 January 1953. Not much of a gathering, not much room either, just enough for my mother to cope with the cooking. I think we were able to seat ten people, including Tina, who had been my letter-writing sweetheart all through my days in the RAF and was now in pride of place at my side. As far as I remember, there was no singing, apart from 'Happy Birthday' of course when the cake was produced. There was plenty of jollity and I was the butt of most of the jokes flying around from my pals.

I knew about the present, a watch, which I was to receive from my parents because I went to the jewellers with them to make sure it was the one I wanted. It was the same jeweller in Argyll arcade that we were to buy our engagement ring from years later. The choice was between a Zenith and a Zodiac watch with little difference between them. I chose the Zodiac because it had a small circle containing the little second hand and I think I made the right choice as it is still on my wrist to this day, despite trips to countless jewellers over the years. The watch cost a princely 15 guineas, but when you add in all those visits to various jewellers over sixty-five years for inspections, glass replacement, springs renewal, servicing and cleaning I reckon that its original price has increased by well over £2,000. Why didn't I just get a new digital watch? Never! Even though I have to remember to wind it up every night, the pleasure I've derived from it takes me back to that day in 1953 when it was bought for me with so much love by my parents.

It was now 1954 and Tina and I had become engaged. My father was obviously happy, because he knew a man, who knew a man who was a jeweller in the Arcade and who got us a great deal on the solitaire. Dad was great; he always knew somebody.

Tina was now travelling to work on the train from Tollcross. My father was always down at the station first and he would stand on the platform, where he could see the train coming as it left Carmyle and wave us down Corbett Street. The harder he waved, the quicker we ran. Tina used to knit on the journey; in fact, she was always knitting. We would pick up more friends at the next stop, which was Parkhead. I would pull the strap at the window, and lower it down, to let them know where to find us. Genuine this time, unlike those Sunday night excursions 'doon the watter'. There were intermittent gaps of light as the train passed between the high walls until we picked up the rest of the gang at Bridgeton. From there on, it was low-level all the way into Central station. That was a relatively clean journey, unlike the return at half past five where, after missing our usual train, which we often did, we would have to endure crowded, dirty and poorly lit compartments. That was because the later train was packed with workers coming home from Clydebank before continuing on its journey all the way to Whifflet after dropping us off at Tollcross.

Now that we were engaged it set the seal on our future happiness. It would be a few years before we were married as we had to save, save, save. In the meantime, we carried on with our usual activities: the tennis, the choir, the merry eight, and, because it was approaching winter, badminton, which filled a huge part of our calendar. We were in three clubs: the Edrom Street badminton club, Bluevale badminton club and Drumover church badminton club. All of them played to a different standard, Edrom being the highest followed by the other two in descending order. Tina, of course, was always first-team standard and, in Edrom Street, that was very high. I took a more carefree approach, treating it as a pastime rather than a dedication.

The thing I loved of course was the walk home after the badminton. Bluevale was farthest away but after we got past Parkhead Forge, it wasn't long before we reached the chip shop at the corner of Edrom Street. We were regular customers; it was where we got our fritter fix on Tuesday and Thursday nights. They sold the best fritters in Shettleston, which we would devour with relish, replenishing the energy we had used up on the badminton court. We walked all the way along Wellshot Road till we got to . . . yes, you've guessed it, our winching spot in the close at 66 Altyre Street. That was my little bit of heaven, while Tina's mind might be wandering back; why didn't I play a drop shot in that last game that could have won the second? Oh, come on, concentrate Tina. Just one more kiss.

We were now an established couple in the eyes of our friends. They knew it was going to happen sometime, the sparkler on her finger being the clincher. It was 1955 and it would be some time before we could think of marriage. The first thing would be finding somewhere to stay, as neither of us wanted to move in with parents. Many questions were asked: when, when, when? Meanwhile life carried on as usual, with Tina showing her worth on the tennis and badminton courts and me doing my best to keep up with her. It didn't affect our love and we enjoyed playing at our own levels. Deerpark choir and the Merry Eight was the equaliser, as I was in charge in that department.

My drumming career

You will have seen various references to the Clan Macrae Society pipe band. This is the story of my journey to becoming a member. Ever since I was a child I was drumming mad. Anything which made a noise that resembled a drum, I would bang. My grandad made me a small pair of drumsticks, either of which could become an imaginary sword when the need arose. I have already mentioned my grandad accidentally knocking me down as he entered the house.

Leaving that mishap aside, let me bring my father in. He went through some musical phases, one of which was learning to play the coronet. He joined the Beardmore cadet brass band and would be constantly practising a tune called 'Juanita' at home, until my mother could stand it no longer. Even today when that song is played on the radio, I can still hear those grating sounds coming into my head. My mother eventually managed to persuade him to give up that hobby. He then became a member of Stewarts and Lloyds pipe band, in which he played the bass drum, an unlikely choice of instrument for someone who was only five foot two. He could hardly see over the top of it but was a good player. While he was in the band, he would listen to the side drummers (or the kettle drummers) and the rudimentary exercises he picked up from them, during their practices, he passed on to me.

Daddy, mammy, daddy, mammy, if, when beat out slowly with alternate hands, each drumstick could eventually be speeded up to produce a drum roll. Paradiddles were next. LRLL, RLRR, LRLL and so on. Mastering those, I was soon able to rattle out a beat and enjoy drumming along to pipe tunes. I would go anywhere to hear a pipe band; the ultimate pleasure was when we went to Dunoon at the end of August for the Cowal games.

One Saturday, I was in George Square watching a parade in which many good bands were passing. I had been standing on steps leading to downstairs offices and I became so excited that my foot slipped over the edge and I fell into the lower basement. I can't remember how long I was down there. All I remember was getting to my feet, staggering up the stairs and out onto the pavement. I was dizzy and had a large, sore lump on my fore-head. I knew my mother was helping my aunt in her newsagents in Cathcart, so I made my way there with the sound of the pipes ringing in my ears. I was made to lie down and had hot and cold compresses applied until I recovered. Falling from such a height, it's lucky I didn't do any serious damage.

Undeterred by my fall I continued to look around to find band practices where I could introduce myself. I went into a dismal downstairs area in Parkhead where a band called the Caber Feidh practised. That visit came to nothing as they were preparing for a contest and didn't have much time for me that day. It was then I decided I needed proper drumming lessons. I had heard of a drummer, Alec McCormick, who lived not too far away. Alec was the leading drummer in the Glasgow police pipe band and there was no better man to approach. I took the bull by the horns, or perhaps I should say the drumsticks by the hands, and went to his house.

'Do you give drumming lessons?' I tentatively inquired.

Whether he just took pity on me because of my innocence or even my height I don't know, but he asked me in. Out came the ironing board and a hard rubber pad mounted on a block of wood was placed on top, the perfect surface for practice.

'Okay show me what you know.'

I went through my exercises and a little bit of a march which included my drum roll and a paradiddle or two. Before I left home, my mother had told me to ask the man what the lessons would cost. When I asked the question, Alec laughed. He must have been impressed with what I had shown him because he asked me to come back next week at the same time. Alec was on regular points duty at Parkhead Cross but, as luck would have it, this was his day off. It was the beginning of a wonderful association between tutor and pupil, one in which money was never mentioned. Through time, I was treated almost as part of his family, but a few years later they emigrated to Australia and we lost touch. It was a pity because I regarded Alec and his family with much affection.

Under Alec's tuition, I was now learning to read drum music, adding strange-sounding things like flams, drags, semi-quavers and demi-semiquavers into my repertoire. I joined Rutherglen pipe band, having been given a good recommendation for Alec. I took part in many contests with them, all the while dragging the long-suffering Tina along with me to contests in places as far apart as Helensburgh and Shotts. The Cowal games, of course, was on the itinerary.

The band came high on the list of prize-winners and even achieved first place in one contest. But Rutherglen was still second grade and therefore would never be able to win a world championship. To achieve that I would have to become a member of a band in first grade. However, there were so many bands in the first-grade category that achieving world-championship status would require a huge amount of dedication by the band I chose to join, plus a great deal of luck on my part. I applied to become a member of the Clan Macrae Society pipe band, which I had long admired, and more importantly, was in first grade. I was grateful to be accepted into their ranks with open arms.

Still no feather bonnets but at least the chance to make it to the top.

House hunting

Tina and I were thinking about somewhere to live when we got married, and, my mother, conscious of that, began to look at the possibilities. There was a single lady who lived downstairs called Miss Booth who died around that time and her house, a single end, was put on the market at £75. 'That would be a perfect wee house to begin your married life,' my mother thought, but we wanted something a bit bigger.

Our search continued until we came upon the perfect place: a two-room-and-kitchen with bathroom and spacious hall, together with a small room with bunker. It was three stairs up, with two houses to each landing, in a beautiful red-sandstone building at 49 Craigmillar Road in Battlefield. We had found our dream home at last. What made it even more desirable for me was the wonderful skylight, which meant that the landing could double as a studio, if, of course, our as-yet-unknown neighbour across the landing agreed. There was only one problem – the price, which was £450. When my mother heard this, she nearly had a fit. 'Where are you going to find that kind of money?' was her first reaction, no doubt thinking about the single-end downstairs at £75.

My father gave me the name of a solicitor he knew and trusted, by the name of Lyndsay Orr, but first we had to approach the bank for a loan. This was the first time I (or Tina for that matter) had to sit facing a formally dressed bank manager with a stern look on his face. This man held our future in his hands. You could have heard my knees knocking halfway down the street.

'Let me see now, you want a loan of £450?' I imagined him saying.

'He's never going to give us such a vast amount of money out of his bank,' was the thought in my mind.

However, the meeting went according to his plan. The arrangement was that we would pay £50 down and £3 11s per month thereafter for twenty years. At that moment, he seemed like a nice man. Hugging was not something that men did in those days but I was tempted. I resisted the temptation till we were outside. 'Weee!', I thought, we've made it. Tina, on the other hand, being more practical, accepted the outcome as if it was a forgone conclusion. You've probably gathered by now that Tina, unlike me, was the one with a head for figures. That's why she became the family bookkeeper after we were married.

Our wedding service was on 5 September 1957, in the Methodist church on Shettleston Road presided over by the minister, the Reverend Mr Sealy. Tina had attended Sunday school and Bible class at that church because her grandfather had been a well-respected member there since his youth and even had the privilege of his own padded seat as repayment for his contribution to the fabric of the church. Tina's sister Margaret was the maid of honour and my best man was a friend, Alec Hair, whom I knew from our train-travelling days. Our parents were at the service of course but the church was remarkably empty. Tina's father was a man of few words but he had a loud voice. After we were pronounced man and wife, his voice resounded throughout the empty church.

'Ye've had it noo Bernardini,' he boomed. Uncalled for, as this remark was, I remember thinking that during all those self-controlled winchin' days, I hadn't even 'had it'.

We had chosen September because we were told by someone who knew about these things that it was a good time to derive a tax benefit. Tina, as I've said, was the one with the head for figures. Anything to do with money I didn't want to know, and that was the way it was throughout our married life. She used to keep a red school jotter (which I still hold dear), where she recorded our weekly spend in those old pounds, shillings and pence columns.

Right down to the last halfpenny.

Earning a Living

When I left Whitehill at fifteen, I had to find a job. The only thing that I was good at was drawing. I trudged around town, clutching my sample book of watercolours, trying anywhere that might need an artist. I remember walking into a printer's and speaking to a man in overalls. I asked to see to the boss, shouting over the noise of the printing machines.

'What is it ye want son?'

'Do you need any artists?' I shouted.

'Dae we need ony artists Wullie?'

Wullie was the man in charge, and recognising that I was clueless about what went on there, he decided to humour me.

'Let's see some o' yer work then son.'

I showed them a couple of examples. Obviously impressed with what he had seen he shouted to the fellow I met on entry.

'Haw John. Come oan ower here an' see this boy's work.'

Both he and John must have been impressed by the standard of my work. They sent me on my way but not before wishing me luck and telling me they wouldn't be surprised if one day they saw my work in the Scottish Academy. After more unsuccessful attempts at finding someone who would be interested in taking on a watercolour painter, I went home dejected. My father, meanwhile, knew a man in the GEC called Addie Drysdale, who had been in the Navy with a friend who had an advertising agency in town. Armed with this contact, I made an appointment with the man who bore the impressive name of R. N. MacDonald Menzies, ex RNVR. I was granted an interview with him and his father, Peter A. Menzies, and they didn't take long to reach a decision. I was taken on as an artist at the princely sum of £1 a week. This was to be my dream place of work from the age of 15.

It was great to be away from school at last and doing something I loved. It was also the first time I had ever worn a suit with long trousers. The suit was bought at Weaver to Wearer, at the corner of Argyle Street and Stockwell Street, at a cost of £4 10s. On payday a single £1 note used to be tantalisingly floated down in front of me like a falling leaf by the stern cashier, Miss Shorthouse. (One cheeky lad on the staff used to refer to her by a similar-sounding name, best left out of these pages.) It took me all my time to trap that note on the desk and stuff it into my pocket to take home to my mother. She took fifteen shillings, while I was allowed to keep five shillings.

During the working day, I was answerable to Ken MacLaren, the production manager, who hailed from Dundee and would often come out with amusing Dundonian expressions. One such expression was, 'Div eh sut punk?', which translates as 'Do I suit pink?' Mr McLaren wasn't an artist, so I got to do all the little drawings of ex-army gear that would appear in the ads for Robert's Stores of Argyle Street, one of our clients. This was the start of an enjoyable career. It was my university. I couldn't wait to get home to show my mother the drawings, which regularly appeared in the *Evening Times*.

The company, P.A.M, paid an annual bonus and I'll never forget the time I was called in to receive mine. Peter A., the man himself, was behind the desk dressed in his kilt. Proud to be the chief of the Menzies clan, he wore it every day to work. He handed me a thick envelope with a curt, 'there ye are son, there's a wee bonus'. I knew what the envelope contained, as I had taken it into the office toilet for a sneak preview.

When I got home my mother was preparing dinner. I told her about the bonus. 'Oh aye, that was good.' When she turned around, I opened the envelope and counted the money slowly.

'That's ten, twenty, thirty, forty . . . fifty.'

My mother nearly dropped my plate.

'Sixty, seventy, eighty, ninety.'

She must have thought Christmas had come. She was standing there, speechless. I'm sure that whatever she used the money for, I benefitted in no small way, but that wasn't the point. It was such a thrill for me to see the look on her face and I felt like a millionaire handing over such a huge windfall.

The agency was given voucher copies of all of the papers and magazines in which their ads appeared and this amounted to a lot of paper throughout the year. Every so often we would have a clear-out and the staff would benefit once again by sharing the money when these printed copies were sold for waste paper. Not a great amount, but another good bit of pocket money all the same.

After two years of national service in the RAF, I was now back working at P.A.M. The agency had secured many new accounts in my absence, one of which was Stuart & Stuart of Charing Cross.

Before I left to serve the King, a Mr Miller worked for the company and he was still seated at the same desk as if those last two years had never happened. He was a small man, always immaculately dressed in striped trousers, a black jacket and waistcoat, with watch chain slung between his waistcoat pockets. To complete the ensemble, he wore a black homburg hat and obligatory umbrella, which were carefully hung on the large curly coat-stand when he got to work in the morning to sit at his desk with the gas fire behind. He was the epitome of a high-flying London city gentleman, although he must have been at least 65. I'm sure he was kept on the staff out of pity, rather than for his contribution to the agency's work. Mr Miller only seemed to look after two small classified accounts, and one other, which happened to be his pride and joy. It was a company that sold a brand of headache powder called UNEEDA (you need a powder, get it). He was a grandfather figure to me and when his petite wife visited the office, she looked like a lovely granny, making them a matching pair. Yes, the office had a family atmosphere about it in those days.

Talking about the King, I had the doubtful privilege of serving two monarchs. King George V1 died in February 1952, while I was still in the RAF, so it was doffing hats for the King and three cheers for the Queen. Her Coronation wasn't until 1953 but more about that later.

Elizabeth II was on the throne now, and every pillar box had been remodelled with ERII on the front instead of GRVI. This didn't go down well with the SNP, who claimed that she wasn't the second Queen Elizabeth of Scotland but the first. I was so imbued with this notion – thanks to Ken McLaren – that I could easily have been persuaded to slip a wee bomb into one of these offending pillar boxes. As I didn't know anybody who could make a bomb, I gave up the idea and settled for the safer option. I carried a copy of the Scottish Covenant everywhere I went, even to dances, urging people to sign it, losing a few friends into the bargain, but still managing to retain my group of faithful pals including the Merry Eight.

I was well into tennis by now. While I never had a hope of reaching first-team standard, I was quite content to be one of the many who played at Deerpark. Tina was doing well, swinging away in style, and in one of her matches the umpire was Eddie Mitchell, my pal you may remember, from the time when we had the idea of building a tunnel between our houses. Eddie was one of Tina's partners in the mixed doubles and became one of my rivals for Tina's affections while I was away on National Service. I was thankful that my true love stayed true and was there for me on my return.

We had one new client, Scottish Land Development. We ran a series of full-page ads in both *Scotland's Magazine* and in *Scottish Field*. These demanded full-colour illustrations showing their earthmoving equipment, alongside various places run by the National Trust for Scotland. I was given the job of painting the first illustration of the Caledonian canal, and there were to be many more scenes throughout the course of the campaign. The agency must have wondered why they gave me the job, as it meant that I became 'artist in residence' for a whole week, to the detriment of work that had to be put aside, while this ad was prepared. A freelance artist who was very good at figure drawing, David Anderson, was called upon to draw the man and tractor that appeared in most of the subsequent ads. Needless to say, P.A.M. couldn't afford to have me spend weeks at a time enjoying myself, painting pretty pictures all day. We soon came to an agreement that I was allowed to work on them at home on a freelance basis. This suited both parties and it got the day-to-day work done.

One of the clients at P.A.M. was Central Bridge Jewellers, whose shop was under the Central Bridge. Their six-inch, double column ads in the *Citizen* and the *Times* were crammed full of drawings of rings with prices ranging from £5 to £25. As they needed extra shop staff in the run-up up to Christmas, we were asked if we'd like to stand in on Saturday afternoons to help out. I got Tina to come in as well as we could use the extra £2 10*s* that Oscar Hill, the owner, was offering. Oscar was short and stout and wore a dark suit and waistcoat, which, as he had a fag permanently attached to his lower lip, was always snow-white all down the front. The shop was always full of customer and there were nearly as many assistants behind the glass-topped counters. Oscar made sure that these were carefully divided, by a strip of Sellotape, into sections before the rush started, and this was our allotted space, which we were only allowed to leave if we were taking money to the cashiers at each corner of the U-shaped counters. I liked it that way. It meant I didn't have to deal with money and I could be sure I was giving the customer the correct change.

One day, a customer asked to see a watch and I duly showed him a selection. One of them was an oblong-shaped piece with no dial and only two spaces, one for the time and one for the date; something like today's digital watches. When asked how it worked, I immediately got into sales mode and did my best to assure him that this was the latest technology, hoping that he wouldn't ask any more questions. Now this new-fangled piece of gold-looking apparatus cost a whopping fifteen guineas (or £15.75 in today's money), the use of guineas to price the watch made it seem much more valuable. 'I'll take it,' he said. Money handed over, the deal was done. It was only at the end of the day that I realised I had made Oscar a happy man, as the profit was much more than your common or garden engagement ring. Oscar stood in front of the staff, blowing white ash all over his waistcoat, and hung an imaginary medal round my neck. (It would have been too much to ask for a real one.) Oscar's pronouncement was, 'Walter that was a good deal already.' We were happy to be going home with another fiver for the wedding pot.

In the early 1950s, Peter A. Menzies moved premises to 2 Newton Place, close to Charing Cross, a large corner house on three floors, with reception room, attic rooms and basement. It sounds as if there were acres of space but with the move came more staff and more clients too.

One of the most prestigious clients was Elders of Charing Cross, which sold contemporary furniture, including Cumbrae bookcases, the Boomerang chair and the Bambi chair. The illustrations all had to be drawn, which suited me of course, because in those days photography in advertising wasn't that common, especially in the newspapers. The Bambi chair was a very interesting product; it was made from a long, flat, rectangular shape consisting of four pieces of different woods that were laminated for strength, then pushed into a machine that steamed, cut and bent it into the shape of the finished chair. It might look here as if I'm promoting the product, which I'm not, because the chairs, together with the company, have long since been consigned to history.

There was one source of embarrassment during my time at P.A.M. Because we didn't have a bath at home I had to visit to the public baths once a week. In order to conceal this from my colleagues, I put my towel in the large pocket of my raincoat and when it was time to leave, I would change my mode of transport to catch the no. 1 bus for Sandyhills outside the office door. I would then get off at Shettleston and walk up to Wellshot public baths, before walking home through Tollcross park. This routine seems ridiculous today but I didn't want anyone to know we didn't have a bath at home. Human nature, I guess.

Marriage

Our wedding

The Royal restaurant in West Nile Street was the chosen venue for our wedding breakfast, or should I say dinner. The only people attending were the best man, Alec Hair, the maid of honour, Tina's sister Margaret, my mother and father and Tina's mother and us of course. Tina's father didn't attend as he preferred the local pub (each to his own, as they say). The evening was rounded off by the guests, all five of them, going off to the Alhambra to see the *Five Past Eight* show. We left to go home and, after changing, were off on our honeymoon at last. It was a rush to get to Central station for the 9.35 sleeper to London. Train journeys were long, drawn-out affairs in those days so from there we had to board another train, which took us to Bristol's Temple Meade station. From there, the last change of train took us to our final destination, Torquay.

It was a new experience signing the register at our bed-and-breakfast as Mr and Mrs, as many of you will recall. The proprietor there could never cope with our name and it was cause for a quiet chuckle every time he asked, 'porridge or cornflakes, Mrs ehh?', followed by 'porridge or cornflakes Mr ehh?'

We soon got used to being Mr and Mrs ehh in that part of the world but *we* knew who we were and we were so happy to be on life's journey together at last. Torquay lived up to its reputation as part of the English Riviera and while we were there we visited many of the towns on that coast including Paignton, Brixton and Babbacombe, which is truly a model village. There was another attraction we had never seen before: a railway that went up a hill, called a funicular. Hardly a novelty these days, but something we had to have a go on and the views from the top were spectacular. We also took the opportunity to visit Plymouth and stand on the Hoe, where Sir Francis Drake had reputedly played bowls as he waited for the tide to change before engaging the Spanish armada. We saw ships, boats and yachts of all shapes and sizes but unfortunately no Spanish galleons.

In Plymouth there was clear evidence of the bombing the town had suffered during the war. We had never seen so many people on crutches and in wheelchairs, and that brought it home to us. We went to Babbacombe a couple of times and it was there that we made our first purchase for our new home in the form of a carved African figure, which we lovingly christened Charlie Babbacombe. Another day we paid a visit to a local fair, where I saw a forlorn donkey standing alone in a field. I thought it deserved a wee clap, but before I knew it he had opened his jaw wide and clamped his teeth firmly on my hand. He wouldn't let go. Was this his way of saying 'be my friend'? It didn't feel like it. I had to stand there while my dear wife looked on, trans-fixed, while her new husband had his hand chewed off. The donkey finally decided to release it, possibly because I was belt-ing him with my free hand. All's well that ends well, except for a badly bruised hand. I wasn't worried. I now had a wife to kiss it better.

There was a friend of my father, Frank Lane, who used to live in Garrowhill with his wife Doris. He had played in the same water-polo team at Shettleston baths. I knew them as aunt Doris and uncle Frank. I loved to visit them for two reasons. One was because he had served in the Middle East and had war books from that period, which kept me engrossed while they chatted. The second was the large, preserved red-admiral butterfly fixed to the mirror in the sitting room; I was fascinated by it and wondered if it would ever take off and fly round the room.

Frank and Doris had moved to Paignton and my father told me to be sure and visit them as they weren't too far from Torquay. This we did, and were made very welcome at their boarding house. If we had only thought of it beforehand, we could have booked up with them instead of at 'Mr ehh and Mrs ehh's' place in Torquay. We spent a lovely afternoon and evening with Doris and Frank and while we were there, they took us to visit their local, a beautiful, traditional English pub. It was our first time in a pub, but a memorable part of our honeymoon.

I knew it was the custom for the groom to carry his bride over the threshold but having to carry the cases over was enough. Anyway, I had done the bridegroom thing before we left, when we had rushed back to change for the journey. Charlie was unpacked first and placed on the mantelpiece for the time being, and then we got down to unloading everything else. We hadn't taken delivery of the large and small wardrobes yet, so everything, apart from our dirty washing, was strewn around. My mum and dad had set up the bed and made sure we had food but, as we wanted to take our time in choosing our dining-room suite, a wedding present from my folks, which wouldn't come until later, the only furniture we came back to was a Minty armchair, a present from Peter Menzies and an Eastcraft tea trolley, a present from Alec, our best man. When its top was swivelled and opened out it became a card table with green baize. Meanwhile, covered with a tablecloth, it became our dining table until we chose the real thing.

We got home on the Saturday and I'll never forget the first Sunday breakfast Tina made. She was so determined to prove that I hadn't just married a pretty face, but someone who knew how to please her man in the gastronomic department as well. Rather than tell you what was on the plate, it would be simpler if I told you what was left off it – and that was the proverbial kitchen sink. She scaled this lavish offering down in succeeding weeks I'm glad to say, but she had proved her point.

I wasn't going to starve.

Our new house

We had a house to decorate and furnish, which was going to be exciting first-time round. All those rooms, all those walls and ceilings to be papered and painted. Having learned how to hang paper when I lived at home with my parents, I thought it was going to be straightforward. As I worked opposite Sanderson's it was easy for me to nip over and take my time in choosing the right paper. The only problem was the papers that appealed to me were often the most expensive. I was in charge of design, while Mrs Moneybags could quickly bring me down to earth with her big red book.

'Okay, I love the colours in this one, and that one is gorgeous but look at the prices,' she would say.

'Och, but Tina, that one is . . .'

'No. We can't afford it and that's that.'

Married life is all about compromise and this was my first lesson. I ended up using a combination of emulsion paint on three walls, one or two rolls of the expensive stuff in the bed recess in the living room, instead of six, and emulsion for the rest of the room, which was all in at the time.

We bought our dining-room suite from Morris of Glasgow and because of the agency connection we managed to go easy on Mum and Dad, whose present it was, by securing a staff discount on a beautiful Meredew suite. It had an African-walnut dining table with black legs, a centre swing-up extension and six black-ebony wooden dining chairs, which I chose to have covered with the same fabric in a different colour. I did a count on the total number of colours in the living room and it came to twenty-six. That may sound like a lot but I can assure you everything blended perfectly.

We were settling in nicely and getting to know our immediate neighbours. There was a lovely lady in the flat across the landing, who became a very nice neighbour. We referred to her as Miss Brown. That was the way it was in those days, out of respect for a lady who wasn't married. We never got to know her first name in all the years we lived there.

We were fully occupied in decorating and furnishing the house every evening and at weekends. Tina was back in her old job at McDonald and Morrison's tea merchants in James Watt Street, while I was at my new desk on the first floor at Peter A. Menzies.

Having finished the kitchen and the living room we started on the rest of the house. This took all our energy but was made all the more pleasurable, as I enlisted the help of Alec, my best man, who willingly lent a hand at the weekends. We managed to secure a bunker space round the back, which served a double purpose. It not only freed up the coal hole, as we called it, off our main hall, after the dirty job of clearing it out was done, but also saved the coalman the job of carrying his heavy sacks up three lots of stairs. I'm sure he was grateful.

That small coal hole was eventually converted into a dark-room, where I could indulge my hobby of photography. The only problem was that I had to carry the wet, newly fixed prints quickly through the hall each time to the bathroom, where they would dry. In due course, I managed to put the darkroom to good use financially, as I got the job of official photographer at the GEC dances and places like that. Everybody always wanted to have their 'photie took' at functions in the days before selfies were the norm. Tina would take the orders while I took the pictures. We got used to having all these strangers in the house, being hung out to dry above our bath.

Gradually, we got to know the district. We were lucky to have a dairy around the corner, on Lochleven Road, which was handy for milk, eggs, ham and the like. It was run by a man called Thomson, whom we got to know. Again, no first names. It was always Mr Thomson.

We now had our bedroom furniture installed, a large and a small wardrobe and bedside cabinets, which had the brand name of Stag. The makers, I can't recall. The only room left to complete was the front room but that would have to wait because funds were low, even with the photographic business. At lunchtime Tina walked from her office in James Watt Street and we would usually eat upstairs at Copeland and Lye in Sauchiehall Street, where they did a good lunch for something like 2s 9d (about 14p, those were the days). We would buy our dinner for the evening, which Tina cooked to her usual high standard. We managed to acquire an old telly, which had a blurry oval within the small screen, and lived with it until we could afford a better one.

It was winter now, and the priority, at least for Tina, was to find a badminton club close to home. The Congregational church on Cathcart Road fitted the bill nicely and provided the opportunity, not only to continue with much-needed sporting activity during the winter, but also to widen our circle of acquaintances. We were soon accepted into the club and quickly got to know and enjoy their company.

One person we got to know very well was an office bearer in the church, as well as a member of the badminton club, who lived alone in Cartvale Road. We both liked Jimmy a lot and he would often end up in our house after the badminton. If the conversation got to a personal level, his manner suggested someone who was deeply distressed and he appeared most disgruntled when he talked about his work. He was employed in Glasgow Corporation's accounts department in John Street, and it became obvious to us that he was in a rut. He would make his way home from our house in an outwardly cheerful mood but he was a troubled soul.

This was the first New Year in our new house. The front room still wasn't furnished or decorated so we just shut the door and forgot about it for now. Earlier in the day we had mentioned to Miss Brown from across the landing that as we weren't going out she would be welcome to be our first foot. Sure enough, after my usual routine, open door, step outside, knock door, and welcome across the threshold by my own wife, there was just enough time for the 'gie oot, tak in' dram nonsense, before Miss Brown and her friend were at the door. Shortly after we heard another knock and who should it be but Jimmy, accompanied by Jean from the badminton club – a close neighbour of his – and her pal, also from the badminton club. Thankfully, because of a wedding present, we had enough glasses to cater for our unexpected guests and so our first, traditional New Year at Craigmillar Road was an enjoyable, if somewhat reserved, gathering of new friends.

New Year celebrations were now behind us and one night while the badminton was in progress we had a visit from the minister. This was the first time I had seen him or even knew who he was. I had just come off the court and was introduced to him.

'Walter, this is Mr Bateman, the minister.'

I knew he had already met Tina as I had seen them talking on the platform during my game.

'You're new to Battlefield. How do you like it here?'

This was followed by a few more questions, to which he already knew the answers. I kept waiting for religion to come up but my wait was in vain. It was never mentioned; everything else but, in fact. Even his parting words were 'well, enjoy your evening'. When we got home, we had a chat and came to the same conclusion – we liked the man. Tina had been brought up as a

119

Methodist and me in the Church of Scotland and even though we had been married under the Methodist flag attending a local church didn't seem like a big deal. Mr Bateman's easy-going manner made the decision easy and from now on it would be the Congregational Church, one of many Protestant denominations. To me, it was just another club. After all I had joined the men's club, the camera club and now Tina was in *the* club.

'You might have waited,' was my mother's immediate response to the news that Tina was pregnant.

'Waited for what?' was my immediate reply.

'Well I mean, a wee bit longer.'

I wondered if all mothers were like this. She should have been thankful that we had waited till we were married; otherwise she would have had a scandal on her hands. Think what the neighbours would have said. We had to smile at her response and so did she when she realised she was going to be a granny. We still had the front room to finish and now, with this news, we had an addition to allow for in the bedroom.

In those early days, nothing much changed. I was working harder than ever, being in sole charge of two more clients, Walker's sugar, which meant client meetings both in the agency and also in Greenock where I did the pack-design presentation. I enjoyed working with Walker's because my contact there, Mr Alexander, was very agreeable. He took me to lunch in the Malmaison restaurant in the Central hotel, very posh for me at that time but most enjoyable. Scottish Machine Tool Corporation – for whom I designed countless brochures – was my other responsibility and the man in charge there was Alfred Bennie. His father had designed the Bennie rail plane, which in those days could be seen at Milngavie on its elevated section of rail. I still have a hall stand after all these years, a wedding present from Alfred.

That year our first holiday was to Dunoon where I was kept busy sketching and painting. I would even send them home as cards, trusting that the rain wouldn't spoil them as they were painted in watercolour. It was during that holiday, imbued with a certain Highland spirit, that I decided to have a kilt made by a tailor on the main street. A bad decision as it turned out. While the muted Caledonia tartan was perfect, especially for someone with the name Bernardini, I realised when it was delivered that I had made a big mistake. I should have waited till I got home and gone to Lawrie's or Henderson's. They, no doubt, would have corrected the look and the hang of it by adding a couple of extra pleats. As I was being constantly reminded, only I would notice the difference.

Tina, on the other hand, spent her time clicking away with those four small needles to produce baby items. I could never understand how four needles could produce such woolly wonders, although I had some experience of knitting. At school, as part of the war effort, me and the other boys would knit blankets for the men at sea. We only had two needles and we used them to knit squares, which were later joined up into blankets. We tried our best but you could have pushed your fingers through the holes we left in some of those squares. I used to think, 'God help them on the Murmansk convoy'.

Tina and I were able to enjoy each other's company at lunch every day, as she was still at work and would be almost until 'D day'. She had been a knitter as long as I had known her. Jumpers and other such items being hurriedly rolled up with the needles stuck through them for depositing in the bag when it was time to move. Now her focus was wee socks and matinee coats, which were guaranteed to draw many 'aws' from admiring ladies.

Every Sunday morning, we went to church. Mr Bateman was a real influence as we both enjoyed his sermons, which were very natural and didn't feel like religion being rammed down your throat. The older people in the congregation were pleasant and helpful. Mr Millar, one of the older gentlemen, heard that I needed a large artist's easel collected from Kelvinside and without hesitation offered his van. This was just one example of the friendliness extended to us, the new kids on the block.

At home, the front room was taking shape and I had extended the mantle shelf from the central fireplace to run along to the end wall with locally gathered stone running in parallel underneath. That made a great difference and I was able to display my model aeroplanes, made from the new Airfix kits. They were so much simpler than those wooden chunks that had to be sanded to shape and which I could never master, unlike my cousin Jim in Lloyd Avenue. There was a great wee model shop along Battlefield Road where I would buy the latest kit and spend winter evenings making and painting them. Mr Thomson, the man who owned the dairy around the corner, saw some of them and asked me if I would like to display them in the window. He was so nice that I couldn't refuse but I still wonder what interest they would have to women buying groceries. I don't know what happened to those models but someone must have got a masterpiece of a replica Sunderland flying boat.

Victoria Road was a great place to shop without having to go all the way into town, which we saw enough of during the week. There were always nice wee items on offer, and we added them to our growing collection of bric-a-brac. Some of them would have either been broken, or ditched, through time but one item we bought in a shop – on the right-hand side as you face town – proved to be precious. It was a plate, nothing fancy, just something that attracted our attention. It still hangs, pride of place, up there alongside Charlie Babbacombe of course. I liked it so much that I incorporated, and duplicated it, into a still life with peppers. On the walk home, I would always buy another wee Airfix kit to work on, while Tina went to play badminton. Yes, she was still playing in another club on a Saturday.

I should say her and her precious package growing inside.

Starting a family

It was now the twenty-fifth of October, and, back home from a visit to Tollcross, the first signs of the imminent birth became obvious. The suitcase packed, we called the ambulance and were driven to Robroyston hospital. I was asked to leave as it was still the early stages but the next day, just after three, I got a brief call to tell me that Tina had given birth to a baby girl, mother and daughter both doing well. I grabbed my things and scurried off to the hospital.

As it was Sunday, there were no florists open but I picked up a bunch of roses at the hospital entrance and proudly strutted into ward B, where Tina was cradling a little bundle. All I could see was a wee, wrinkled, blotchy red face and a shock of black hair peeping over the tightly wrapped bundle. Surely that's not ours, I thought; none of us have black hair. Judging by the number of other men with black hair at their wives' bedside, my first thought was that they must have got the babies mixed up.

'Well done love. I've brought you these . . .'

Before I could get the word 'roses' out of my mouth, they were taken away by a nurse to be put into a vase alongside the many other floral tributes brought that night. Once I had become accustomed to this wrinkled bundle of humanity, which was ours, and even been allowed to hold it rather nervously for a couple of minutes, I knew that at last we were a family. Just as we were saying goodbye I was approached by a large, smiling, black-faced nurse who said 'come with me young man'. I had no idea what she wanted, but as she had also propositioned some of the other fathers, I soon realised that we were being taken down the corridor to give blood. A small price to pay for what our wives had gone through for hours.

'Take me. I'm yours,' I said, holding out my arm in submission.

A lot of everyday tasks were added to our daily routine now that we had a baby to look after. Being three stairs up, it fell to me to take care of the first one. We had been given a pram by Tina's sister May, which she no longer required, and it was as good as new, so that saved us a few bob. Bumping it down the stairs each morning, then bumping it all the way up at the end of the day, would at least keep me fit. I was spared the job of preparing bottles in the middle of the night as Tina was able to cater well in that department. The only problem was that she would wake me up at four-hour intervals so I could watch. Only joking!

Elma, who was Tina's ladies-doubles partner from their days together in Deerpark tennis club, now lived in Govanhill Street, which wasn't too far away. She had given birth to a son, Colin, a few months earlier and her and Tina would meet up at Queen's Park gates to go for walks when the weather was nice. Elma recalls the day that Tina was late and, not sure what to do, decided to walk in the direction of Victoria hospital. When she reached Battlefield Rest, Tina was walking towards her in a distressed state.

'Sorry I'm late, but I dropped Linsey.'

'What? You dropped her?'

Elma thought she meant the baby had been dropped from a great height, but fortunately that wasn't the case. Tina had been changing Linsey on her knee and while she was opening the nappy pin (anybody remember them?) Linsey had decided to roll off, ending up on the floor. She had a pronounced bump on her wee head and for Tina, a young mum, it was traumatic. Nothing of a serious nature, thank goodness. Nothing that a wee cup of tea down at Victoria Road wouldn't cure. And that's exactly what they did.

In May 1962, we had our second child. This time it was a home birth attended by the district nurse, otherwise known as the 'green lady'. Not surprisingly, as their name suggests, they were always dressed in green with matching hats, carrying their bag of tricks as they went on their rounds. Fiona was the girl assigned to us. We were given her telephone number, and when Tina's labour pains were about twenty minutes apart, we contacted her and waited, and waited . . . and waited.

It was only when the pains were down to ten-minute intervals that the front-door bell rang. She had judged it correctly but lost no time in preparing for the birth. Fiona made sure I had laid out plenty of freshly boiled water together with towels and everything else she would need. As her assistant, I made sure I carried out her instructions to the letter and we were getting along fine until it was time for Tina to go into the bedroom. The door was closed behind them and I was told to stay out. It was four in the morning and Fiona, and Tina for that matter, were on overtime; it was bite-my-nails-and-wring-my-hands-time. At five o' clock precisely, after many agonizing groans, I heard the first little cries and at exactly the same time I heard the dawn chorus from the birds outside, which fitted the occasion nicely. Oh tea! I hastily prepared a cup and knocked on the bedroom door. Fiona was having none of it.

'Bugger off. You're far too early,' she shouted.

'Boy or girl?' I asked.

'It's a girl and Tina and baby are fine. I'll tell you when it's time.'

It was the twelfth of May.

My night in the pulpit

As I mentioned before, I was impressed by the way the minister of the Congregational church in Battlefield delivered his sermons and also his down-to-earth manner. Although I wasn't a manager of the church he persuaded me to deliver a sermon at the manager's evening service, which was an annual event. This was a shock but, at the same time, always up for a challenge, I accepted his offer. I had never thought I was capable of climbing up into a pulpit to deliver an oration of this magnitude but as the time grew near I got used to the idea. After all it would be similar to my stage appearances. Mr

Bateman gave me some pointers, which helped me to put the sermon together. While taking his advice on board, and using quotations from the Bible for emphasis, I preferred to go down a more humanitarian route, one centred on peace and harmony.

The year was 1962 and I had plenty to work with.

I began my sermon by noting that America and Russia were busily expanding their nuclear arsenals and that the Cuban missile crisis had nearly precipitated World War Three. The Cold War, I noted, hung over us like a cloud; the year before, Russia, with a great deal of propaganda, unleashed the destructive power of a 50-megaton hydrogen test bomb. It was the biggest bang the world had ever known. I said it was ironic to think that the nuclear age began with a device that became known to the people of India as the 'Christian bomb'. I was in full flow now, turning to the southern states of America, and the segregation of black children on school buses as a manifestation of the power of white over black.

These were a few of the incidents I touched on before getting down to issues nearer to home. I resisted the temptation to lean forward with one arm over the pulpit, in ministerial gesture; I felt it would be overdoing the power I was enjoying up there in his pulpit. I rambled on until I got back to issues that came under the peace-and-harmony theme. I condemned not only the animosity between Rangers and Celtic but also the mild forms of what would later become known as racism. People didn't applaud in church in those days but as I stepped down to resume my seat, I felt I had reached the congregation in a way that would make them think about how they treated their neighbours. At the end of the service, Mr Bateman shook me warmly by the hand, reassuring me that I hadn't dishonoured his pulpit.

Married life

I was happy enough playing tennis at the courts belonging to Weirs of Cathcart, the engineering company. The courts were down beside the river Cart and I recall many people who worked there. Tina and Elma became members of Kingswood, which was high up in the leagues and more suited to their standard. For the first time in their tennis careers their partnership was split up and they had to get used to new partners in league matches. Naturally enough, this didn't go down well with either of them but Kingswood refused to split their first couple as they were a winning combination. This would be understandable to anyone other than our two girls and was cause for long discussions between them after the tennis had finished.

'Where have you been till this time?' would be my retort when Tina came in.

'Oh, we were just talking.'

I had been babysitting of course and I was happy to accept her reply as I knew they would endlessly go over the evening's play till the cold of the evening caught up with them.

Linsey was usually out for the count when she was put down for the night. I would always be busy making another aeroplane model or perhaps drawing. One night, I went through to check, and couldn't resist sketching her in this dishevelled state before covering her up again for the night.

The church and its social amenities took up much of our time. Badminton of course, the ladies' club, the men's indoor-bowling club and the photographic club were all part of these extracurricular activities. Two pictures, of which I was quite proud, were much applauded during one of their club-night appearances. We regularly attended church, and Linsey was introduced to the Sunday school. The children would be seated at the front of the congregation and Mr Bateman would address them with a suitable story before they were taken into the hall where the Sunday school teachers would take over.

Around the same time, Glasgow Corporation decided to lessen the density of the Greater Glasgow area by decanting much of the populace to outlying areas, East Kilbride and Cumbernauld to name but two. I was given the job of coming up with an idea for the promotion of the week set aside for the exhibition. This was held in the McLellan galleries, incorporating my design of the exhibition itself. Perhaps some of you may recall visiting the exhibition and being inspired by the concept, if not already having been notified of the corporation's intention. The exhibition was called GROW, an acronym of Glasgow Redevelopment and Overspill Week. It was hoped it would be the beginning of a freer and cleaner lifestyle for a great many people. I used Linsey as the model and Central station was the location for the shot. The headline in the advertisement was 'Sheena Wilson is moving' and the copy went on to extol the virtues of the family relocating to the new towns.

Someone, I can't remember who, jolted me out of my complacency by suggesting that I should think about moving jobs. It was 1959 and I had been with Peter A. Menzies for twelve years, including my two years compulsory service in the RAF. It had never crossed my mind to leave P.A.M. as I was happy there. Judging by the reputation I had built up, including becoming a Licentiate of the Society of Industrial Artists, I supposed someone might be interested in hiring me. As it so happened, a man by the name of Douglas Soeder had been following my career and asked if I would like to work for him. He took me to lunch and we discussed the possibility of me joining his graphic-design unit, Forth Studios, which, as its name suggests, was based in Edinburgh. Moving jobs within Glasgow was one thing but moving to Edinburgh would involve too much upheaval for my family. I reluctantly declined his offer.

I was granted another interview by Sommerville & Milne, a well-respected Glasgow agency situated on the corner of Bothwell and St Vincent streets. I accepted their offer of £16 per week, a jump of £3.10s from my current wage. Tina, of course, was thrilled as it made up the deficit in our weekly income since she was no longer working. Our only concern was how P.A.M. would react when I handed in my notice. I needn't have worried as it was accepted straightaway both by Mr Menzies and Mr Hastings, who was by this time a co-director. I wondered why they didn't offer to up my salary in order to keep me. The reason should have been obvious. The different agency managers and directors met every month at the Publicity Club of Glasgow for lunch, where matters relating to their staff would come up in conversation. It was probably in my future interest that they should let me go. In fact, they may even have been wondering why I hadn't handed in my notice earlier.

I began work at S & M in August 1959 as a senior visualiser to the creative head of the art department. It soon became obvious that there was a lack of understanding between the account executives and the creative staff. I found this peculiar, but thought I would get used to it. For instance, when receiving a new brief from the account executives, directors included, I found it difficult to extricate the fine details from them in order to produce the best possible ad. Whether this was because of a lack of communication between the client and the account exec, or whether it was because I wasn't on their wavelength yet, I could only hazard a guess.

There was a carefree attitude among the workforce however, which I enjoyed, and a feeling that they respected my work. We also had a welcome tea break both in the morning and afternoon, when a dumpy wee tea lady called Gertie would appear with her tray. I don't know how she put up with the ribald comments from the boys, but somehow she managed to ignore them and carried on with her daily duties.

I became good friends with a lad called Roy McElwee, who came from Greenock. Our association grew to the extent that, after a while, myself, Tina and Linsey would sometimes take a daytrip down to meet Roy and his wife Betty at the weekend. I am pleased to say that both of us, widowers now, are still in touch, even though he lives in England.

As time passed, I became restless, not because of the jovial atmosphere but for the reasons I mentioned previously. Since I had at last found out how easy it was to move from agency to agency, I proceeded to put the word out that I was on the market again. It didn't take long before I was called for an interview at Rex Publicity, an ad agency located at 10 Claremont Terrace. I had become a licentiate of the Society of Industrial Artists and I'm sure that the suffix LSIA after my name impressed them enough to offer me the position of art director, with a salary of £1,850 a year. I readily accepted and wondered why I didn't get into this moving business earlier.

Rex Publicity was a breath of fresh air, an entirely different atmosphere from S. & M. The creative department was situated on the top floor and next to it was a small room where the creative director, Andy Muir, sat. Before becoming an advertising agency, Rex Publicity was in the business of cinema advertising and produced large posters promoting the latest films. Andy was employed as an artist with that company and he was a good artist – portraiture being his speciality – but he was a good deal older, and clearly not in the same creative world as us keen young go-getters next door. We were a law unto ourselves and we knew it, and thanks to high quality of our work, we were the agency's creative ambassadors.

We sat at individual desks but when one artist was briefed on a new campaign, everyone would be curious as to how he would go about it, while still engaged on their own projects. The freedom we enjoyed as we walked from desk to desk during a break would take our own minds off our own briefs, albeit temporarily. It also meant that we were able to criticise a young associate's efforts in a jocular, but helpful, way with remarks like, 'You're not seriously thinking of putting that in there are you?' This often resulted in a change for the better. I was never afforded that luxury when I was at P. A. M.

While based in Clairmont Gardens, we would sometimes go for lunch in one of the first restaurants owned by Reo Stakis, Le

Chatelet, close to the Charing Cross end of Sauchiehall Street. I had designed the menu, which was subsequently chosen to appear in *Modern Publicity 1962/63*, a design annual featuring the best examples of modern advertising design. Reo Stakis owned many eating houses, both in Glasgow and on the outskirts, including a steak house in Hamilton, for which my cover featured a drawing of a bull's head. The last menu I designed for him and also created the advertisement for its opening was the Dalriada on the Edinburgh Road at Cranhill. I made the ad as exotic as I could by having a photograph taken at night and adding a fireworks' display above the building to enhance the effect.

But let's get back to the Le Chatelet story. I would listen to the orders being called out to the chef and the one I remember best, probably because it was the one asked for most by customers, was 'two moussakas 'n' chips'. This, shouted in a broad Glasgow accent by the waiters, always made me chuckle. When the order was ready we would hear it shouted back at the waiter: 'two moussakas 'n' chips'. We never ceased to be amazed by this; it was so out of keeping for a French-themed restaurant owned by a Greek.

There was a keen golfer in the creative department called David, who would often have his clubs with him and this led to friendly rivalry, as we would use one of his clubs to see who could chip the most balls into the wastepaper basket. Any excuse for a break! If the noise got too much for Andy, his door would open and he would stand there like a patriarch. It would only take one of his characteristic whistles to make us return to our desks. Another well-known phrase of his, when looking for a lost object that might have been purloined from his room was, 'has anybody seen the 'doohicky', or sometimes 'the doomy', and of course always preceded by a whistle. We gently mocked him for these little quirks, behind his back of course. As the agency photographer was constantly in and out of the creative department, someone asked him to capture me doing an impression of 'the whistle'.

Another of the senior art directors I worked with was a friendly competitor by the name of Drew McDonald. Drew was very hirsute, able to grow a moustache almost overnight. The story goes that one night, on a date, it had grown to such an extent that his girlfriend, Audrey, asked, 'Why don't you cut that moustache of yours? Even by half would be better.' So, when he turned up the next night, he did just that; he shaved one side of his face and left the other half with the bushy moustache in place. Would you call that being as 'mad as a hatter' or merely being creative? I think the latter applies.

Drew had started his working life as a house painter and was now in a position where his creativity came to the fore. The agency had some prestigious accounts in its armoury and both Drew and I had the privilege of working on the best of them. We had been issued a directive by the managing director, David Mitchell, to produce award-winning ads. In my case, the opportunity arose when I was assigned the Golden Wonder account. At that time the company was relatively unknown and situated in Sighthill near Edinburgh. I created a little cartoon character, which I named 'Poppacrispin'. This was later to be adapted by Hallas & Batchelor, the London animation company, for television and other media campaigns. In line with the MD's fondness for award-winning material I was fortunate to have two of my Golden Wonder crisps ads chosen to be among the best 100 British ads and consequently was published in the prestigious *Leyton Awards Annual* of 1962. This delighted the MD as well as looking good on my CV.

The practice of collecting good printer's proofs of our ads from the agency became the norm. They could be presented to prospective employers when the need arose. Drew was a master at raiding the vouchers department to add to his collection as he had higher aspirations in mind. If he admired one of my ads he wasn't above borrowing it for his sample book, in exchange for one of his, with the words 'we could easily have done them, couldn't we?' Unfortunately, major international accounts were hard to come by in Scotland; most of them being handled by the so-called big boys down south. Undeterred, the ever-resourceful Drew discovered a back door to London and that was through Dublin. At that time in Ireland, these international accounts were handled within that country's borders. In consequence, we career-hungry designers were given the chance to work on them to add to our portfolios. Once the Dublin door was open, no less than five visualisers from Rex Publicity, including myself, took the same route.

It would mean the beginning of a new life.

We needed a car

At Rex Publicity I became very friendly with Bob Provan. Bob had a car and was very knowledgeable about all things mechanical, an area beyond my comprehension. He was a finished artist, the term used to describe a person whose job it was to translate the visualiser's ideas into workable mechanical drawings for print reproduction. It was largely because of his influence that I thought of buying my own car and we used to spend our lunch break looking at cars in showrooms all over town. I was merely the onlooker, with Bob steering me towards the right choice. This went on for some time and through many lunch breaks if we weren't playing snooker, the regular lunchtime recreation of our group of four from the agency. We had reached an impasse on car-gazing when, one day, a car appeared in a Bothwell Street showroom. As we passed it caught Bob's eye. 'That looks nice. Let's go in,' he said.

It was a four-year-old Austin Cambridge, with 35,000 on the clock and a price tag of £450, just within my budget. It looked in perfect condition and was in two-tone grey, exactly to my taste. After a test drive with Bob at the wheel, he gave it the all clear; I flashed the cheque book and the deal was done. The next morning, Bob drove over to me and left his car outside my house. To get into work we jumped on a bus, my usual mode of transport, but for him something of a novelty, as he hadn't been on one for years. After work, we collected my new purchase from the garage, and he drove it home, with me in the passenger seat. Then off he went in his own car, leaving mine sitting outside the close for Tina and I to gaze on lovingly. Our own car! Learning to drive the thing would be my next adventure.

I couldn't let poor Austin just sit there so I signed up with British Motor School for driving lessons. As luck would have it, my driving instructor lived across the road, which was very handy. Now it was time for my first lesson. Press clutch to floor, into first gear, release handbrake, check mirror, release clutch, press accelerator and we're off. Oops, stalled. Handbrake! So many things to remember. 'I'll never get the hang of this,' I thought. I'm sure all you drivers can relate to that reassuring tone the instructor had learned to impart, even when he was knotted up inside. It wasn't long before you were hearing those words in your sleep and repeating them to yourself when you were behind the wheel. I couldn't wait for the next lesson.

Bob was my other instructor. He would drive over at weekends and take me out for unofficial lessons. His style was informal and full of humour, unlike the guy whose job it was to notch up another pass. We were out on the road one day when Bob said, 'Just slow down here, mirror, signal, pull in, brake, handbrake. Done! Just you wait here.' After a little while he got back in the car and exclaimed, 'Ah that's better.' He had been on a quick visit to a gent's he knew was around the corner. I might have known. It was Bob at his best. Was this a driving lesson or a lavatory tour? It wasn't something you found in the driving instructor's manual. He could always raise a laugh in a serious situation could our Bob.

I could never tell where my extra lessons would take us but one day we ended up at a house in a district of Glasgow I wasn't familiar with. It turned out this was where he lived. We went upstairs and into his house; any excuse for a coffee and temporary relief for Bob's nerves after the drive across town. The first thing that met me was his pet tortoise, crawling around the floor. 'Careful. Oh, I should have warned you. This is Joe,' Bob said. Thank goodness I spotted Joe first, otherwise it might have been tortoise soup that night. The next surprise I got was a friendly tail-wagging welcome from his other pet, Ben, a lovely big Alsatian. It's a good job I wasn't scared of animals no matter their size. Having met his parents and suitably refreshed, it was back on the road again. More instructions from Bob.

'Turn left, a roundabout just up ahead.'

'Roundabout?' I thought. This wasn't something my professional instructor had let me tackle.

But with Bob's careful guidance I negotiated it to his satisfaction. Home again and another cup of tea; Tina had seen me parking, giving her plenty of time to boil the kettle. That was another Saturday afternoon well spent, and, after downing his cuppa, Bob was on his way, pleased that he'd brought me home to Tina in one piece.

Let me bring all this talk about driving lessons to an end by telling you that I passed my test first time. I then used all the information I'd gathered, together with the quiet, reassuring, driving-instructor tones that I picked up from my BMS instructor, to teach Tina. I am pleased to say she also passed first time, which meant that Austin now belonged to both of us.

Islay

It was 1961 and another holiday was due. I had always wanted to visit one of the Inner Hebrides and I decided on Islay. I had consulted Tina and she was happy to go along with my suggestion. Linsey didn't have any say in the matter as she was only two-and-a-half at the time. We flew from Renfrew and it was the first time I had been on a twin-engine Dakota. It was noisy of course, and, although we were all seated facing the front of the aircraft, I couldn't help thinking about those paratroopers on D-day, sitting in two rows facing each other in the same type of aircraft, wondering what lay ahead.

I was brought back to reality as we approached the landing strip, which was situated not far from the sea, between two worryingly close hills. After a brief, but friendly, check to make sure we were the same people who boarded the aircraft half-an-hour ago, we were shown out under a corrugated roof, past a group of people waiting to board our recently vacated plane for the return flight to Glasgow. Oh. my goodness, that must have been the terminal building we just passed through. But this was Islay, not one of your posh airports, and all the friendlier for it.

Happy to have arrived, we boarded the bus for Bowmore, our base for the next two weeks. We lodged with a lovely couple and stayed above their wee shop, which, as if by magic, turned into a pub at night. The house was situated directly off the main street, which ran up from the harbour. I did a painting of Bowmore from the pier (which has been reproduced in the plate section). It is interesting to note that the cows, which you see at the top of the street in my picture, would wander freely in and out of the lovely wee, round church. We used to wonder who mucked it out before Sunday service!

We were lucky to meet up with a couple from England, who owned a car. They kindly offered to take us to Port Ellen for the day, a beautiful little town at the south end of the island. When we got back, and had put Linsey to bed, we went downstairs to the well-stocked bar and chatted with our hosts about our day over a dram. As I've already said, we weren't big pubgoers, but somehow the cosy atmosphere and the friendly Highland accents of our hosts made having a whisky liqueur or two the most natural thing in the world.

The next day, we took advantage of the island's bus service to take us north to the little town of Port Askaig, before boarding the ferry for Jura, where we observed at close quarters the two peaks that are a distinguishing feature of the island. Impressive though they were, I think they are best viewed from a distance where they could truly live up to their more common name: the Paps of Jura.

We had become friendly with our downstairs neighbours in Craigmillar Road, Mr and Mrs McFarlane. He was a rep for Long John whisky and it so happened he was on a sales visit to Islay that coincided with our holiday. He kindly offered to let us tag along as he did his calls and after he picked us up we went with him on his rounds. One call, to the island of Gigha, proved more daunting than the others. It involved being hoisted onto a vessel from a small boat at sea, with the reverse procedure on the return journey. I can't recall the exact details of this little trip but it was exciting, and, I'm pleased to report, without serious incident.

During our stay on Islay, we learned of a ceilidh that was to be held at a village called Bruichladdich at the other side of Lochindaal, (the sea loch on which Bowmore is situated). On hearing this, our kind hostess insisted we should go, promising that she would regularly look in on Linsey. It was too good an offer to refuse and she even arranged a lift there and back with a couple of her friends who were also going. Dancing all night to an accordion band was great fun and a new experience. Between the dances, there were solo singers who, of course, sang mostly in Gaelic, giving us haunting renditions of their island songs.

The ceilidh over, we were dropped off in the early hours of the morning to a darkened house. After bidding a grateful good night to our newly made friends, we crept up the stairs and into our room, where, thank goodness, we found Linsey sound asleep. It had been a wonderful night and a wonderful holiday too, one that lived in our memories for many years to come. While we were there, it had been impossible for me to ignore the peat bogs, which were all over Islay. When I got home, I took my easel out to the landing and used the wonderful daylight from the skylight to transform the many sketches I had made into one semi-abstract oil painting on canvas.

A New Life

Tour of Scotland

Things on the domestic front were running smoothly now and not much was to change over the next few months. Hogmanay had come and gone. We held our usual celebrations of course. Our good friends Hannah and Hugh were there and the party was going with a swing as they first-footed us, removing their helmets and motorcycle gear in the process, as they had arrived on Hugh's motor bike. They didn't have a car at that stage.

We were now into a new year, a year that was to change our lives in ways we couldn't have imagined a year before. In February, Drew McDonald had left Rex Publicity and moved to Ireland, and I was left as senior visualiser. Andy was still in his room as art director, but, as things quietened down after Drew's departure, I could sense a restlessness among the others. Ian, Drew's assistant, was next to leave shortly after that. He was to serve under Drew in the Dublin agency, O' Kennedy Brindley, and stay with him until he could find accommodation.

I was beginning to get itchy feet myself but one thing I felt we must do before we said goodbye to our native land was to see as much of it as we could. This would mean a driving tour, which would mean going around June. With luck, it would allow me enough time to organise the relocation to Ireland before the end of the year. All this planning and I hadn't a job to go to. Was I crazy? You don't have to answer that.

June arrived and we threw everything we needed for the trip into our faithful Austin and headed up the west coast. Everything was going well and everybody was in cheerful holiday spirits. To occupy the girls, and while there were plenty of passing cars, we played a game of looking for number plates in which the first three letters suggested something else. I'm glad to say that the first three on our own car, RVD, didn't appear on any of the vehicles we passed, but there were plenty of others to keep them occupied.

We were between Arrochar and Crianlarich when we encountered a long tailback on a steep incline. After some time at stop-start speed, it was obvious that there had been an accident. As we approached the scene we learned that a tour bus coming down the hill, had toppled over the edge of the road and ended up at the bottom of a deep valley. By the time we arrived, the ambulances were taking on people who were shaken but still able to find their way up from the crash site, with the help of motorists. The more serious stretcher cases were being attended to by the ambulancemen; they took more time to deal with because they had to be lifted carefully out of the bus and up the hill to the next waiting ambulance.

We were soon waved on and on our way again, although it took time and a few cheery songs before the girls could put the shocking experience behind them. We found a nice farmhouse just up the road from the locks at Fort Augustus and spent a lovely night there. Linsey was given a bottle of milk to feed the lambs, which was a great thrill for her but she was also startled by the sheer strength of their suckling.

While continuing our journey up Loch Ness, the girls looked eagerly for signs of Nessie, without any luck. After a while, Linsey gave up and was reading 'The Broons' cartoon strip in the *Sunday Post*, Suddenly, Janis let out a yell; she had spotted a small head poking out of the water. We all knew it was a neck-shaped stick, but to bring the interminable search to a close we managed to convince her that it was Nessie's wee boy Nicky. Happy with that, Janis took to reading 'Oor Wullie'. We were approaching Inverness now and time for lunch. The castle, of course, was the imposing feature there but it wasn't of much interest to the girls, who gave it a cursory glance. After that we did some shopping and looked around for a bed and breakfast.

Elgin was our next stop, where I noted that the cathedral, which must have been impressive in its day, was a sad ruin. Directly opposite, there was a lovely park, where the girls had a good opportunity to let off steam, run around and play on the swings before they were once again locked in the confines of the car.

Ever since I was a small boy, I had always imagined that the map of Scotland resembled Santa Claus. The area to the north of Loch Ness was his upper body, further north to Sutherland and right out to Duncansby Head his red hat. Where we were headed now would be across the top of Santa's sack. Moving further east we came to Macduff, which was our next overnight in a B and B. It was on the left-hand side going east and overlooked the sea. The house was quite small, with a wee narrow stairway leading to the bedrooms, but the cramped accommodation was more than offset by the lovely hostess who was very welcoming, and, like many others on our trip, admired Janis's flowing blonde hair. The other great thing about Macduff was that as we were so far north, we were able to enjoy the remarkable daylight; it lasted until the early hours of the morning and we were lucky enough to witness the brilliance of the Northern Lights.

The next stage of our journey took us over the hump of Santa's sack, bypassing Peterhead and down to Aberdeen. It was while we were there that I found out we weren't going to be rich after all. I had been holding on to a 1924 penny that had been burning a hole in my pocket for ages, and I was convinced that it was one of only a few still in existence. I walked into an antique shop, carefully unwrapped my precious penny and laid it on the counter. 'Well,' said the valuer in response to my hopeful smile, the bland look on his face instantly dashing my hopes. It was a worthless piece of copper with a date that was on thousands, if not millions, of other pennies still in circulation. How come I had never come across any of the others?

Oh well, now that we were on our way again, I had to find the nearest petrol station before heading for the world pipe-band championships, which were being held in Aberdeen. I hoped to catch up with some old cronies, whom I hadn't seen for ages, not since leaving the Clan Macrae Society, the band I was in when we won the world title in 1953. I found them in the corner of the tuning-up area, which had been set aside for that purpose. I shouldn't have been surprised, but the band had many new members, none of whom I recognised. The new boys were surprised to meet one of the original drummers from the 1953 band and I enjoyed chatting with the few remaining members as we recalled those heady days. I was pleased to see that Charlie McIntosh – Snowball to his friends – was still the tenor drummer. He was the smallest man in the band but he certainly knew how to bang that drum.

As we were leaving, the band went into their chosen march, strathspey and reel: 'The Highland Wedding', 'Dornie Ferry' and 'Mrs McPherson of Inveran'. I remember thinking as we left the field that the magical sound we had perfected in the Fifties wasn't quite there anymore, but that might have been wishful thinking. Time to move on, we waved them goodbye. It wasn't until I read the Sunday paper that I found out they weren't among the winners.

Moving down the coast we reached Montrose, where we were to spend our next night. It was a pleasant town, where we had a well-earned rest. There had been heavy rain when we left in the morning but the sun had come out by the time we got to Dundee, looking every inch its song title, 'Bonnie'. While we were taking in the sights, I had an odd encounter with a local woman. We were browsing the shops on the main street and while I was looking in a shop window I saw the reflection of a woman behind me. As she looked me up and down she seemed startled. In those days I always wore shorts on holiday and thought nothing of it, even though it wasn't common in those days. As I turned to face her, she shook her head in revulsion. To our surprise, and those of the people around us, she uttered the words 'bold and brazen' in a loud, reprimanding tone of voice, before striding off. After she had gone Tina and I broke into uncontrollable laughter at her outburst.

Our next stop was Perth and from there I couldn't resist trying to locate Leeside cottage, which was situated about ten miles to the north. As a young boy, I had spent two great holidays there with my parents. The memories came flooding back as we came within sight; it hadn't changed a bit. I stopped the car, walked across the road and knocked on the door, wondering what kind of reception I would get. After some time, a bent and wizened old woman dressed in black with a shawl draped over her shoulder, cautiously opened the door and peered out. It was at this point I wondered whether this was a good idea. After all, it was my memory I wanted to relive and had nothing to do with this old woman. I mumbled my story about having stayed there but I got little response and left with a feeling of guilt that I, a complete stranger, had intruded on her life. At the same time, I couldn't help wondering if this was the same Annie Culbert we had stayed with all those years ago.

Edinburgh was our next port of call. The Scott monument, the castle and, of course, Princes Street were the main attractions. Shopping took up much of the time there, with tartan trinkets and dolls to buy for the girls. I made sure to stop and let the girls listen for the 'one o'clock gun' – a must for us Glaswegian visitors, whilst the residents of Edinburgh or 'Edinbuggers' as we "Weegies" like to call them, carry on regardless. One of many jokes is the one in which a 'gentleman' from Edinburgh arrives in heaven. When asked by St Peter if he had ever done anything he was proud of, he recounted the story of how he had taken the train to Glasgow and when he got off at Queen Street, he began to prance around, shouting, 'Weegies are crap, Weegies are crap.'

'That was a very brave thing to do,' observed St Peter 'and tell me, when was this?'

'A couple of minutes ago,' replied the brave man.

We couldn't leave Edinburgh without paying a visit to the zoo, a highlight, especially for the girls. There were so many animals that fascinated them; it would take a day to recount them all. Suffice to say that besides the large animals, like the giraffes and the elephants, we had to drag them away from the chimp and monkey enclosures before they almost jumped over the fence to get in amongst them.

As there were then no other major attractions in those days, such as the Falkirk wheel or the Kelpies, there was nothing else for it but to get on the Edinburgh Road and drive the last forty-seven miles past the many mining bings and the view of Cumbernauld new town in the distance. Eventually the 'camel,' the 'buffalo' and the 'battleship' over on the Cathkin Braes hove into view and we knew we were nearly home. There would be many things demanding our attention now, not least of which was the impending big move.

The big move

In preparation for what lay ahead, I booked a flight to Dublin to attend a couple of interviews I had lined up. One of these was with Billy Lindsay, a nice Scottish gentleman in charge at O' Kennedy Brindley. However, as Drew McDonald was already established there, he couldn't offer me a job. The other appointment was with Padbury Advertising. The two people who interviewed me there were Mamie Dignam, who owned the firm, and her close relation, Seamus. Despite my extensive portfolio, her main question was about calendars. I thought it a strange question to ask, but I assured her I could design them. I had done one before, at Rex, so I knew it was well within my capability. That clinched it. I was offered the job of senior visualiser, which I accepted. The salary was little more than I was getting at Rex, but it was an 'in' to Dublin. I later learned that her preoccupation with calendars related to the largest account she handled, for Kennedy's, a bread company. Kennedy's produced a calendar every year and it was Mamie's pride and joy.

I returned home with the news that I had been offered a job in Dublin and got a mixed reception. It was finally dawning on Tina that the move was inevitable and that it was time to break the news to family and friends. This was accepted reluctantly in some cases, but accepted nevertheless, in the knowledge that it would be beneficial in the long run, which I felt sure it would be. During our goodbyes, however, I learned that Jimmy, he of the troubled mind, had finally taken a step too far. Whether he was pressured into the action he took by an associate at work we were never to find out, but we later learned that he had been given a prison sentence as a result. This was a situation we could never have envisaged, and it cast a dark shadow over our leaving. It was sad news, something we had to come to terms with.

Later that year I boarded a ship for Dublin, the *North Coast*. I wanted Tina to join me as quickly as possible and set about finding a house for us. By sheer coincidence, the managing director of Scottish Land Development, from my days at Peter Menzies, was also on the *North Coast* that day. I should add that he was in first class, as you might expect, and I doubt if he was seeking employment.

I found accommodation for myself in Dublin easily enough, with a very nice couple; I had a room to myself and was able to dine with them in the evening. They lived a short bus ride from the city centre and I found the journeys a novel experience. Having been brought up as a Protestant, I found it strange that almost everyone around me on the top deck of the bus would suddenly bless themselves at exactly the same time when passing certain side streets. This, I soon realised, was because there was a church at the bottom of these streets. I got into the cheeky habit of watching closely to see if someone knew there was a church hidden away as we passed the next street. Then I would wait to see the reaction of the others as they joined in to bless themselves because they had forgotten about that particular church. Shame on them!

Drew McDonald let me have the use of his car at the weekends and this enabled me to get from one area to another without any problem. At the same time, I was trying to familiarise myself with the thick Dublin accents of the various builders I came into contact with. All that took up a good deal of my time at weekends but it was well worth the effort. Having picked three houses as possibilities out of the many I viewed, I arranged for Tina to fly to Dublin, so that I could whisk her around them in one day. It wasn't easy, but we managed it. There was no doubt about the house we both wanted, which was on a lovely avenue leading down to the sea on Dublin's smart southside. Our first flat in Scotland had cost us £750 and sold for £1,200, while the house we purchased in Dublin cost £3,000. These figures are a good argument for avoiding renting and getting onto the property ladder as quickly as possible.

In the meantime, we corresponded by letter and phone on a daily basis until the travel arrangements had been finalised and the date for the removal set. Moving house from one country to another isn't easy at the best of times but Tina coped with it in an exemplary manner. Everything went according to plan and all I needed to do was to pick up my car from the docks and then drive to Dublin airport for Tina and the girls. We were now ready to meet the removal van at the door of our new house and watch as our worldly possessions were unloaded.

My thirty-year account of those 'dear old Glasgow years' is at an end. By way of an epilogue, I feel I must leave the reader with a few thoughts on the transition. Having made the choice to begin a new life, largely due to personal ambition, it was now up to me to make sure that moving my family from one environment to another, especially another country, was as seamless and stress-free as possible. My daughters took to the change remarkably well; they made friends easily and quickly adapted to their new life. I, too, enjoyed the change and looked forward to furthering my career.

It was Tina who was most affected by the move: shopping proved hard to adjust to with a totally different range of foodstuffs on offer, and, as supermarkets were still to become the norm, the Dublin accent was hard for her to understand when she was talking to the assistants. There was no such thing as sliced sausage in Ireland but there was worse to come. One day, Tina went into the butcher's and committed the cardinal sin of asking for pope's eye steak. You could have knocked the butcher down with a feather! Needless to say, blessings abounded around the shop at this blasphemous utterance. While extradition wasn't on the cards, it certainly came close.

Our official address was now 3 Ardagh Park Gardens. I took the opportunity to paint a shortened version on the pillar at the side of the gate, 3APG, which, for reasons I never understood, became 'THRAPG' to certain people. We were fortunate in having nice neighbours on either side of our detached house and I was happy that through time, we became members of the local tennis and badminton clubs, making integration into the community easier and more enjoyable, especially for Tina.

She gave birth to our third child, Alison Lorna, on 6 January 1965 and our family was now complete. A wonderful wife, three lovely daughters, a new house in a new land and a job that some-day might take me to Madison Avenue (it never did). What more could I ask? Oh aye, just a couple of things – square sausage and a good Scottish mince pie.